CIVIC LITERACY
AND
CITIZEN POWER

James D. Chesney
Henry Ford Health System

Otto Feinstein
Wayne State University

PRENTICE HALL, Upper Saddle River, New Jersey 07458

Library of Congress Cataloging-in-Publication Data

Chesney, James D.
  Building civic literacy and citizen power / JAMES D. CHESNEY, OTTO
  FEINSTEIN.
    p. cm.
  Includes index.
  ISBN 0-13-309741-2
  1. Political participation—United States. 2. United States—
Politics and government. I. Feinstein, Otto, [date].
  II. Title
JK1764.C45   1997

                         324'.0973—dc20   96-23083

Acquisitions editor: Michael Bickerstaff
Editorial director: Charlyce Jones Owen
Editor in chief: Nancy Roberts
Marketing manager: Chaunfayta Hightower
Editorial/production supervision: Edie Riker
Cover director: Jayne Conte
Cover photo: Eugene Gordon
Buyer: Bob Anderson
Editorial assistant: Anita Castro

This book was set in 10/12 Stone Informal by East End Publishing Services
and was printed and bound by Courier Companies, Inc. The cover was printed by
Phoenix Color Corp.

 © 1997 by Prentice-Hall, Inc.
Simon & Schuster/A Viacom Company
Upper Saddle River, New Jersey 07458

Printed in the United States of America

10   9   8   7   6   5   4   3   2   1

ISBN 0-13-309741-2

Prentice-Hall International (UK) Limited, *London*
Prentice-Hall of Australia Pty. Limited, *Sydney*
Prentice-Hall Canada Inc., *Toronto*
Prentice-Hall Hispanoamericana, S.A., *Mexico*
Prentice-Hall of India Private Limited, *New Delhi*
Prentice-Hall of Japan, Inc., *Tokyo*
Simon & Schuster Asia Pte. Ltd., *Singapore*
Editora Prentice-Hall do Brasil, Ltda., *Rio de Janeiro*

CONTENTS

This book is dedicated to our children, who, like their parents, are learning to become citizens. To
Carey Chesney,
Sarah Feinstein,
Tasha Feinstein

PREFACE

There are two concepts that provide our motivation to write this book and underlie its content.

First, politics abhors a vacuum. People who speak can be heard and responded to, even seemingly powerless students can make their voices heard.

Second, politics requires *praxis* (Greek for combining thought and action). Being heard in politics is a matter of thinking (figuring out how to articulate your concerns or how to connect your views with someone else's views) and taking action (speaking out on an issue).

Our goal in this book is to provide you with both an understanding of civic literacy and an action plan that can build your power as a citizen. Each chapter describes what we currently know about the topic and then describes activities that provide a learning environment for civic action.

Our thinking and work on the topic of civic literacy is based on ten years of experience using this approach in political science classes at Wayne State University, with community groups in the Detroit area, and with high school students throughout southeast Michigan. Our largest debt is to the thousands of students, whose articulation, commitment, and concern about politics provided the inspiration and incentive to work on this project.

The Civic Literacy Project benefited from a dedicated cadre of graduate students who found the time and energy to motivate and organize students while pursuing their academic careers. Cynthia Duquette, Shannon McCormick, and Anthony Perry worked throughout the project to challenge students and faculty to political knowledge and participation.

Student contributions have been a vital part of this effort. Elizabeth Agius, Jerome Almond, Rhonda Ateis, Jerrel Cooper, Alvaro Cortes, Pat Dostine, Mary Duncan, Jean Pierce Faletta, Jeff Farrah, Peter Fuller, Elizabeth Holcomb, Chris Koenig, Keith Morris, John Lees, Charo Melesky, Maureen Murphy, Matt Perry, Sara Shepard, Anita Shina, Charles Smith, Kendra Ventour, Richard Wagner, and Jeff Weigrand have contributed their time, intelligence, and enthusiasm to the Civic Literacy Project.

We are grateful for the support of community groups such as The Michigan Ethnic Heritage Studies Center and New Detroit, Inc. Wayne State University through the Office of the President, the Office of Affirmative Action, the College of Urban, Labor, and Metropolitan Affairs, and the Political Science Department provided financial support. Sharon Flowers, Marie McQuarrie, and Dorothy Vasquez provided administrative support from the Political Science Department. Professor Rodolfo Martinez of the WSU School of Education, Michael Donofrio and Germaine Strobel of the Michigan Ethnic Heritage Studies Center, and Chris McElory were all active collaborators in this effort. The Michigan Campus Compact, housed at Michigan State University, contributed funding.

We are grateful to the staff at Prentice Hall. Charlyce Jones Owen encouraged us to write this book; Mike Bickerstaff oversaw the editorial and marketing; and East End Publishing Services turned the manuscript into a book.

Wayne County Commissioner George Cushingberry and Wayne County Clerk Teola P. Hunter provided financial and political support for the Project. George Cushingberry's support extended to the classroom where he combined his doctoral training in political science with his practical knowledge of politics.

Finally, we thank our families and friends who have sacrificed time, money, and attention so we could pursue civic literacy.

CHAPTER 1

The Concept of Civic Literacy

This book is about power.

It is about our power, as citizens, to shape the world we live in or our abdication of power to others who will influence decisions. In politics there is no vacuum. Decisions are made; voices are heard or ignored.

Power is the ability to influence citizens or political institutions. Politics is the use of power. Most books on politics describe whose views are being heard and analyze why. This book is different. We want your voice to be heard. Thus, our goal is to describe how your ideas and those of your fellow citizens can be translated into government action. We want to provide you with the tools of political power.

A government of the people, by the people and for the people, requires a citizenry capable of determining what they want and acting in a way that forces the government to respond accordingly. To be capable, you must understand the democratic political process and know the skills that lead to effective political action. This book describes these processes and skills and presents a series of opportunities for citizen action.

To realize what power we have and how to use that power requires civic literacy. Civic literacy is the ability of citizens to decide what governments *should* be doing, understand what governments *are* doing, and have the skills required so that governments *will* respond appropriately. Resolving the contradiction between normative (what government should do) and empirical (what government does) is necessary in order to determine the role of government. Civic literacy refers to the skills necessary for functioning as a citizen in a modern democratic society.

There are two essential characteristics of civic literacy. First, thinking and action have a synergistic relationship. Civic literacy is an active learning process where ideas are tested and revised through thoughtful action in the political arena. Second, the building blocks of civic literacy are citizens and the civic structure that connects them. Citizens are the components of the political system. The structure is the set of rules that determine how values are allocated and how citizens communicate using political institutions and processes. Civic literacy empowers citizens to use the rules of their political system to meet their needs. Any political action requires knowing the rules. For example, to register voters you have to know the rules and regulations of the voter registration process. (See Chapter 4 for more on this topic.)

Civic literacy is the capacity for conscious political action. Table 1.1 demonstrates how the components of civic literacy are combined.

The civic component of civic literacy consists of citizens and structure. Citizens are the fundamental building blocks for a political system. The way in which those citizens are organized is the structure. The political structure determines how conflicts will be resolved and who will get what, when, where, and how.

The literacy component consists of thinking and action. In the case of reading, for example, the activity of looking at the page is com-

TABLE 1.1 Elements of Civic Literacy

		CIVIC COMPONENT	
		CITIZEN	STRUCTURE
LITERACY COMPONENT	THOUGHT		
	ACTION		

bined with attempting to understand a message. Similarly, in politics, thought and action are combined. A well-conceived political campaign is useless without the action of a candidate running for office.

LITERACY

Literacy requires both a mastery of mechanics such as reading and writing and a conscious or critical attitude when using the skill (Pattison, 1982, p. 177). Simply knowing how to construct an English sentence does not make one literate. To be literate you must construct the sentence AND understand that the words used are a distortion of reality. Words are symbols. Even the alphabet is used differently by different cultures. The Semitic writing system was used by the Phoenicians for business and commerce and by the Hebrews for understanding religion (Pattison, 1982, pp.44–45).

Literacy is closely connected to political power. Pattison observes, "literacy, no matter what its kind, is used for power" (p.83). As an example, he cites the Romans: "The soldier and the grammarian proceeded in lockstep to spread the Roman way, one by conquering the world, the other by providing it with correct Latin as a medium of organization" (p. 83). It is certainly no coincidence that in the period after World War II, American English became the dominant language of international trade and diplomacy. An economic and political superpower can impose its language on the rest of the world today just as the Romans did.

The movement of people into cities was more than a shift in physical location. It represented a major change in culture. It created a society of strangers, of people who do not share the same traditions, histories, and meanings. Our words "metropolis" and "politics" have a common root in the Greek term *polis*, meaning many, the coexistence of many peoples or cultures—the city.

The changes involved in modernization (including urbanization) create not only new needs, but often entirely new social groups not previously part of the social and political system. Since these needs are not part of the political system, they are not responded to and often continue to grow. At some point these unmet needs turn into demands, which put pressure on the political system to respond. The ability to put pressure on the political system requires civic literacy.

These concepts of thought and action of citizens and structures have their roots in the basic works on Athenian democracy published 2,500 years ago. The legacy of Athenian democracy is a system of governing based on enlightened self-management, the rule of law, and nonviolent conflict resolution. The tools for building this system are civic literacy and citizen action. To develop such a method of governance, Athenian philosophers had to understand how human beings perceive, how they learn, and how this process could be harnessed for the purpose of enlightened self-government. To this end, *Book VII* of Plato's *Republic* contains a conversation between Socrates and his friend and relative Glaucon, which describes human nature and the human learning process by means of an analogy to a cave.

In their analogy, humanity lives in a cave, chained to the floor, in fixed positions, seeing shadows created by other human beings. These shadows are taken for reality. By means of communication between the chained slaves, a consensual verification is established further assuring the slaves of the "reality" of their observations.

Somehow, some of the slaves perceive something different than the shadows. To resolve these differences, some slaves break free of the chains and move to the light. When they emerge from the cave and its shadows, they are blinded by the sunlight of reality. As they regain their sight, having now become accustomed to the light, having integrated their experience with reality into their thinking, they return to the cave and their former peers. They are blinded again, this time by the darkness of the cave. The ability to communicate and discuss reality with the cave dwellers is reduced by their experience outside the cave.

In the analogy of the cave, shadows represent our culture; the symbols and the light represent reality. Our access to knowledge is through symbols such as words and numbers. It is by means of these symbols that we have access to the knowledge necessary for our survival. To be useful, the symbols must be clear and precise even though the reality is complex and confusing. Our love of symbols and our distaste for reality are a continuing human contradiction. The processes of education and deliberation, which allow the integration of thought and experience, allow us to live with this contradiction.

The initial blindness in the face of light is the impact of significant learning on the learner. Significant means that it challenges the person's entire symbolic structure. It is felt as confusion or blindness. The process of integration is only completed when the perceptive structure has been transformed or when the new learning has been rejected, allowing the old patterns of perception to reemerge. The blindness of returning to the cave represents the difficulty of the integration of the newly attained insight into the general culture. To convince the cave dwellers of the new reality, one must see things as the slaves do and change the culture of the cave by integrating the new reality into the old culture and its symbols. Such an integration can only be achieved by a continuous interaction between experience, thought, and theory.

STRUCTURE

The clash between old and new cultures is resolved through the political structure. In a democratic society, there are no cultural or political permanent majorities that can claim the right to govern. Democracy implies decisions by a majority vote with due regard to the minority, because tomorrow's majority may include all or part of yesterday's minority.

Political systems differ in the extent to which the structure is open or closed to their citizens. The three basic purposes of an open democratic political structure are: first, to have a set of behaviors, rules, procedures, and institutions that can resolve conflict peacefully and without repression; second, to have the freedom to see where conflicts exist so they can be resolved before the conflicts become unresolvable; and third, to provide legitimacy for our governmental institutions in a world of many religions, each with their own divine authority. This last purpose is central to our own experience with the United States Constitution where cultural and religious conflict resulted in a political structure designed to provide stability without a permanent majority.

David Hackett Fischer presents convincing evidence that the U.S. Constitution is based on this concept because it was designed to institutionalize conflict resolution procedures for four ethnic groups in colonial America (Fischer, 1989).

After identifying four distinct cultures in the American colonies, Fischer states, "The Constitution of 1787 was an attempt to write the rules of engagement among these regional republics of British North America. The purpose of the constitutional convention was to create an institutional consensus within which four regional cultures could agree to respect their various differences. In the convention itself, some of the most important compromises were not between states or sections or ideologies, but between cultural regions." (Fischer, 1989, p.829) Our basic political structure is the result of compromises between divergent cultures on issues such as slavery/race, taxes, economic policy, freedom, and law. The multicultural conflicts resolved in the Constitution have resulted in a structure in which groups that were previously excluded can fight their way into the political system much as the backwater settlers did with the election of Andrew Jackson (Fischer, 1989, p.849). More recently, forty years of nocratic party control in the House of Representatives ended in 1994 with the election of a Republican majority representing previously unrepresented groups. Elections from 1996 to 2000 will determine which coalition, if any, can create a stable governing system.

Political structures, such as the Constitution, are important precisely because they articulate the rules that are used to resolve political conflict. The U.S. Constitution is a structure that is sufficiently complex, with three independently selected branches and a multilayered federal system, to protect political minorities. This complex structure determines what political opportunities are available to our citizens and what skills they need.

ELEMENTS OF CIVIC LITERACY

Table 1.2 shows how the components of civic literacy fit together. The four elements of civic literacy are opinions, knowledge, deliberation, and participation.

Opinions are individually thought-out views on political issues and people. The first step toward civic literacy (outlined in Chapter 2) is translating an individual concern into a political issue. You must be aware of the connection between your personal needs and the political system. For example, if you hit a pothole or are stuck in a traffic jam on the way to school or work, you may want local governments to spend more money on roads. If you are a student or have a child in school, you are likely to support funding for education. When asked what they wanted for their school, Detroit middle-school students translated individual concerns into policy issues by responding, "textbooks and metal detectors." In this context, individual needs are clearly translated into a political issue.

TABLE 1.2 Elements of Civic Literacy

| | | CIVIC COMPONENT | |
		CITIZEN	STRUCTURE
LITERACY COMPONENT	**THOUGHT**	opinions	knowledge
	ACTION	deliberation	participation

The link between public opinion and public policy is elaborated in Chapter 7, which describes a mechanism that can build closer connections between opinions and policy.

Knowledge refers to systematic thoughts. In politics, understanding the content and process of government action requires facts and analysis. Facts are the building blocks without which political action is either impossible or random. The right to vote, for example, is not useful if you don't know who the candidates are or why they are running for office. Analysis requires linking opinions with each other and with facts. People are more likely to have an opinion if they have an understanding of what the government is currently doing (see Chapter 7). In his writing, Philip Converse shows that the ability to connect policy issues such as civil rights and welfare is dependent on information (Converse, 1964).

The first step in any political activity is the development of a strategic plan. Strategies are built on political knowledge. The strategy for building a voter education campaign (see Chapter 4) requires understanding of how voters use information, which channels of communication are more or less effective, and what issues are important to voters. Acquiring knowledge is fundamental to building civic literacy.

Deliberation is communication with others about political ideas. In a deliberative process needs are shared and analyzed and options are debated. If needs are analyzed and not shared, there is no progress. Deliberation requires the action of meeting with others to discuss needs and to agree on solutions that address the needs identified. Once a solution is agreed to, deliberation with new groups and individuals is necessary to expand support for the solution (see Chapter 3). Deliberation is an important element of any voter education campaign. In Chapter 5 we conclude that **in politics, talk, is action**.

One of the most critical tools of deliberative democracy is agenda building, in which divergent groups come together to agree on the problems and find constructive solutions. The sharing of needs and the analysis of problems by people from different cultures and with different experiences is at the heart of deliberative democracy. Such discussion is critical in translating political thoughts into action, which in turn modifies one's point of view. Agenda building requires special environments and skills, which are presented in Chapter 2.

Participation is taking action within the political structure. For example, raising money to help you run for office requires action within a specific set of rules. In most states, candidates are required to form **Candidate Committees**. The committee accepts contributions and makes expenditures on behalf of the candidate. To ensure that the money is raised and spent properly, campaign finance laws regulate who may contribute, how much they may contribute, how expenditures are made, and what reports must be filed. Anyone running for office must know and follow these rules.

Each element of civic literacy is present in all political activity. For example, running for office requires a citizen to have **opinions** on issues; talk to friends about the issues and possibility of running for office (**deliberation**); acquire **knowledge**, such as information on issues and process of running for office (such as when are the filing deadlines and how many signatures are needed to be on the ballot), and take action by filing proper nomination forms (**participation**).

The political activities outlined in this book also draw on the components of civic literacy. The agenda-building activity outlined in Chapter 2 requires opinions, which are first shared in a deliberative process and then structured and combined with others' opinions through a set of political rules outlining student participation. Voter registration, education, and mobilization (Chapters 4, 5, and 6) are all dependent on opinions (views on various issues), deliberation (discussion of these issues), knowledge (understanding how to register voters), and participation (actually contacting voters).

The elimination (or at least reduced effectiveness) of intermediate political structures such as political parties, community organizations, or powerful neighborhood organizations as institutions that nurtured and screened issues and candidates has placed a heavy burden on citizens to interact directly and evaluate these candidates and issues. As a part of the structure atrophied, new mechanisms have taken their place. Increasingly, the training of citizens in the skills of civic literacy has fallen to special interest groups. Although educational institutions are mandated and financed to provide this service, they have rejected their responsibility by teaching information—not skills.

Setting your own agenda of the issues you feel must be addressed and having the ability to listen to the agenda of others has never been easy, but modern television has made it even more difficult by taking on two political functions best reserved for citizens. The first is in deciding what the agenda is and powerfully communicating it to both leaders and citizens. The second is that of being a critic with no responsibility to offer constructive solutions or alternatives to policy problems. In taking on these functions, the media has turned deliberative democracy into a spectator sport where citizens look at symbols and shadows.

The recent resurgence of studies on democracy can teach us a great deal about the process, effectiveness, preconditions, and values that are necessary to link people and their governing institutions. These studies have not, however, turned that knowledge into opportunities for the practice of democracy. For democratic skills cannot be learned theoretically; they must be mastered through active learning. Learning about politics requires direct interaction with other citizens and with the political structure.

The development, in the past decade, of community service education has opened up the possibility of making civic literacy a part of courses in American government, as well as courses in community organization and social action. Voluntary action and community service require the same skills as political action. In both cases, skills can only be mastered through active learning. Active learning requires direct interaction with other citizens, with community groups, and with the political structure.

This book is devoted to building civic literacy skills, which are necessary for a working democracy, by suggesting a series of activities that can be used in a wide variety of settings ranging from educational institutions to political and community groups. By pinpointing the activities necessary for citizenship, we hope to promote their transmission to a generation of citizens operating in a new political culture.

Citizen power and civic literacy can be built through a multistep process in which people come together to discuss issues of common concern, ratify each others' concerns, build political power by recruiting new voters, hold job interviews with candidates, mobilize and inform voters during the election campaign, monitor the performance of elected officials, and revise the agenda.

Each chapter describes what we currently know about the topic and then describes activities that provide a learning base for civic action. Each chapter thus addresses the components of civic literacy presented in Table 1.1. The final chapter examines the skills that are necessary for civic literacy.

ACTIVITIES

The activities that will help students and citizens understand the concepts from this chapter are:

ACTIVITY 2.1: Building an Agenda Face to Face

As a group, you and your classmates should share your views on what issues require immediate attention and how they relate to each other.

ACTIVITY 2.2: Building an Agenda from Negotiation

The task here is to pool the issues you develop in the face-to-face agenda process to formulate an issues agenda for a larger group.

ACTIVITY 2.3: Building an Agenda Using Telecommunications

The Agenda Convention is ideal for learning how to use the electronic media.

ACTIVITY 3.1: Finding Coalition Partners

The coalition effort can take two routes: one is through your friends and relatives and the other is through your formal contacts with private and public organizations.

ACTIVITY 3.2: Building a Coalition: Agreeing on Strategies and Tactics

Having identified potential coalition partners, you must now discuss and implement a strategy for building a coalition.

ACTIVITY 3.3: Bringing Elected Officials and Units of Local Government into the Coalition

Since governmental institutions set policy agendas, strategies to bring these entities into the agenda coalition are essential.

ACTIVITY 4.1: Analysis and Change of State Voter Registration Laws

An analysis of the state's voter registration legislation and administration is conducted. You will need this information to plan voter registration drives and voter mobilization projects.

ACTIVITY 4.2: Voter Registration Drives

The activity provides an easy first step into politics. It combines taking action (asking someone to register to vote) with information (knowing the requirements for registration).

ACTIVITY 5.1: Voter Education: Informational Pamphlets and Tapes

Prepare flyers, brochures, and videos that explain ballot proposals, summarize candidate positions, or explain how and where to vote.

ACTIVITY 5.2: Voter Education: Candidate Job Interviews

Students interview candidates in a format similar to a job interview for use on local television systems including public access cable.

ACTIVITY 6.1: Voter Mobilization Project

This project establishes Voter Education and Participation Centers in host organizations such as churches, senior citizen centers, neighborhood centers, union halls, shopping centers and stores.

ACTIVITY 6.2: Student Campaign Involvement Project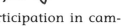

This activity creates opportunities for voter participation in campaigns, parties, or issue movements.

ACTIVITY 7.1: Create an Accountability Catalyst

This action creates an accountability catalyst by recruiting community leaders to develop an agenda and hold candidate forums.

CHAPTER 2

Agenda Building and Acceptance

There is consensus in the modern world that there is one major certainty—change. Change is occurring in how and where we work, how we think and feel, and how we relate to each other as individuals and nations. Change is occurring in what we know, what we need to know, and how we communicate knowledge. Most importantly, change is occurring in who is involved in making decisions regarding the governance of change. Those who govern change determine who reaps the benefits and who bears the burdens of change.

The basic political questions are: how are these changes managed? Whose values are protected or rejected? How are scarce resources distributed? What mechanisms make these decisions and resolve these conflicts? The answers to these questions depend on the structure of the political system and the civic literacy skills available to comprehend and use those structures.

Although change is certain, the elements of civic literacy (**opinions**, **knowledge**, **deliberation**, and **participation**) are stable and are essential tools for managing change. The core of civic literacy is the conscious use of political structures to resolve conflicts and manage change. The structures and conflicts themselves are subject to great changes. As political structures change, the tactics we use to participate in the political system also change. For example, the passage of the 19th Amendment granting women suffrage changed how women participated in the political system but did not change the skills needed to participate. The skills needed to influence elections were the same as those that generated protests and political pressure to win the right to vote.

Changes not only create new political needs, they also create new groups, which are not part of the current political system and therefore have little or no power. Translation of a need into a demand requires organized collective action. When there is organized collective action, these unmet needs become demands, which put pressure on the political system to respond. This pressure requires an agenda to separate the needs that will be acted on from those that will be ignored. It is the ability to shape such an agenda that is the topic of this chapter. The next chapter explores how to build a coalition necessary for the agenda to be acted on.

The most important decision any group of citizens or governmental institution can make is listing the problems it will consider for action. This list of problems is the agenda. Setting an agenda requires a body to choose, off a larger list, the problems it wants to address. Which of the following issues deserve governmental action: health care reform, racism, urban blight, drugs and substance abuse, ethnic conflict, proliferation of nuclear power to new nations, or funding construction of a new baseball park in Detroit?

Agenda building requires the four elements of civic literacy: **opinion**, **deliberation**, **knowledge**, and **participation**. Having an opinion on an issue, sharing that opinion with others, becoming knowledgeable about both your issue and the agenda process, and participating in political efforts to gain attention for the issue are steps in moving from citizen concern to government action.

Democratic politics requires deliberative procedures that allow citizens with vastly different experiences to discuss and analyze their needs. Agenda building is a process whereby individuals or groups come together to agree on their common problems and the order in which they have to be addressed by the political system. Building an agenda requires specific skills and a deliberative democratic structure.

Agenda building resolves conflict between those demanding a response on an issue and those who either want no response on the issue or who are promoting another competing issue for government action. Limited resources, including time for deliberation, make conflict over the agenda inevitable.

The existing constellation of forces determines how new needs and groups will be dealt with by the political system. Very often new needs are not recognized by existing groups. If collectively organized needs are ignored, conflict arises. The existing institutional system then responds by accommodation, or repression, or a combination of repression and accommodation. Agenda building is the process of confronting these issues and determining responses to the conflicts generated by change.

FROM PRIVATE TO PUBLIC CONCERNS

An item is placed on the political agenda when a private concern becomes a public concern (Baumgartner and Jones, 1993, p.27). This process requires the four elements of civic literacy. The starting point is citizen **opinions,** which must be carefully thought out and articulated. Citizens must also understand the rules by which agendas are formed in order to create effective strategies for issue inclusion (**knowledge**). Agenda building combines awareness of a problem with talking and listening to others within an organized collective activity (**deliberation**). Finally, the central activity of agenda building is **participation,** which builds a collective awareness of problems and takes action to bring those problems to the attention of other citizens and public institutions.

Studies of agenda setting often have an undemocratic flavor. Terms such as elite democracy and comments on the lack of political participation and the uninformed nature of the public's opinions are often used as a starting place for these discussions (Cobb and Elder, 1972, p.3; and Coleman 1957, p.9). Jack Walker has used the term "mobilization of bias" to refer to how a consensus of elites controls the agenda (Walker, 1966, p.292).

The apparent lack of democracy in agenda setting is viewed as an opportunity by E.E. Schattschneider, who notes that a large disinterested public can be mobilized to action by those who have been unsuccessful in getting their item on the agenda. Activists can expand the scope of conflict in order to reverse their political fortunes (1960). In this context, Cobb and Elder view agenda building as conflict management. They state, "The study of agenda building is concerned with the identification and specification of the types of issue conflict that receive the attention and action of governmental decision-makers." (Cobb and Elder, 1972, p.63)

The three prerequisites for an issue to be placed on the agenda are: widespread awareness of a problem, shared concern by a large number of people that the problem requires action, and a shared view that the problem is appropriate for governmental action (Cobb and Elder, 1972, p.86).

The conversion of an issue from a private concern to a public concern is a function of political leadership. The essential characteristic of political leadership is the ability to articulate shared goals that bind the leader and followers in a symbiotic relationship (Wills, 1994). When goals are shared the distinction between leaders and followers becomes unimportant. From the standpoint of democratic theory, the leader's power comes from his or her followers and their shared vision. Everybody wins and has power.

Leadership also requires two kinds of knowledge. One is strategic knowledge about how to build an agenda and how and where to communicate it so that other groups and governmental institutions listen. The other is information and analysis on each of the issues to be discussed for inclusion on the agenda. The discussion of issues at the deliberative stage requires facts and analysis, which are used to clarify and build support for an issue's inclusion on the agenda.

BUILDING *YOUR* AGENDA

Most studies of agenda building focus on describing the process whereby a society and its institutions choose to deal with (or ignore) a problem. Unlike previous discussions of agendas, our focus is on how citizens can learn to influence the agenda. The topics for the remainder of this chapter are framed as questions:

- Is there a cycle to the agenda process?

- How can individual citizens or groups of citizens influence the agenda?

- What are the mechanisms that translate individual concerns into shared views and from shared views to public agenda items?

AGENDA CYCLES

There are two seasons in the agenda building process. One is the cycle of political seasons for citizens and the other is the electoral-governing cycle of politics.

The political seasons of the agenda setting process for citizens are open and closed. The open season starts a month after an election is over and lasts for about three years (one-and-a-half years in the case of the U.S. Congress). During this open season, the agenda must gain support from groups, leaders, other citizens, and the media. The agenda season closes with the first primary election. After the primaries, everything is viewed as a horse race. Attention shifts to who is ahead in the polls or delegate counts and what image candidates are projecting. At this point the agenda is forced to address the candidates and the media rather than the candidates focusing on the agenda.

The seasons of those seeking election are linked to the cycle of governing and elections identified by Richard Fenno in his study of legislative careers. Fenno examines the careers for U. S. senators and divides their activity into a cycle of campaigning—governing—campaigning (Fenno, 1991, p.xiii). The transition from campaigning to governing requires the politician to use the just-concluded election as a guide to governing activity during the next term. The transition from governing back to campaigning requires a credible explanation of governing experiences and accomplishments in relation to the agenda put forth in the last election. Michigan Governor John Engler's 1994 campaign slogan, "Promises Made, Promises Kept," captures this concept.

The opportunity to place an issue on a politician's agenda for governing action is greatest before the process of campaigning and election. The issue of health care reform in 1992 illustrates how this process works. The 1990 election of Senator Harris Wolford was viewed by politicians as evidence of the power of health care reform as a political issue, and therefore worthy of national political debate. President Bush and Governor Clinton articulated very different definitions of the problems, images, and solutions to health care reform (Clinton, 1992 and Sullivan, 1992). Health care policy maps were closely aligned to each candidate's overall electoral strategy. President Bush used the health care issue to argue for market, as opposed to government, solutions, while Governor Clinton used the issue as an appeal to economic vulnerability of the middle class and the domestic policy failures of Republican administrations. The link between candidate image and issues is discussed further in Chapter 5.

During the open season, political events can push items on or off the agenda. In 1995, the election of a Republican-controlled Congress pushed health care reform off and put welfare reform on the political agenda. The bombing of the federal building in Oklahoma City put antiterrorism legislation on the congressional agenda and took off a repeal of the assault weapon ban proposed by the National Rifle Association.

As soon as one election is over, the hunt is on for new issues that can mobilize voters in the next election. The search for new issues, or a redefinition of old issues, opens up the agenda building process. During the governing phase of a career, the politician is looking for new issues that can hold or expand his or her election constituency. In his book about Senator Dan Quayle, Richard Fenno shows how the issue of job-training programs could both expand the senator's constituency and reinforce the loyalty of his current supporters. Senator Quayle used the renewal of the job-training program to court support with black and urban voters and to reinforce his ties to the business community. His speeches on the subject stressed the need for these programs in urban areas as well as the need for a government-business partnership (Fenno, 1989).

There is a third cycle you need to be aware of to have influence on the agenda setting process. James Stimson argues that regimes (defined as periods of either liberal or conservative policy direction) always fail (Stimson, 1991, p. 29). They fail for three reasons: 1.) implementation is delayed, 2.) policy reactions are measured after the fact, and 3.) the perception of failure cumulates over time. A concrete example of this phenomenon occurs in models that predict the outcome of presidential elections. These models typically include a factor for the duration of the party's time in power. If a party has been in power more than eight years, the chance of change increases dramatically (Abramowitz, 1988). A second example of this phenomenon is the 1994 ouster of Democrats from control of the House of Representatives after forty years in power.

Regime failure results in issue cycles. The lag between policy implementation and public reaction produces a severe public reaction. By the time the public knows it does not want a program, it has already been implemented and expanded several times.

The best opportunity to add an issue to the public agenda occurs when the agenda cycle (elections—governing—elections) and issue cycles are matched. Mobilizing voter discontent on an issue such as health care during an election can result in an opportunity to influence directly the government's response as either a senator or president. The opportunity to raise health care reform was greater after eight years of inaction by the Reagan administration than at the end of the Johnson administration, which passed Medicare and Medicaid.

Statements of problems are the least likely to be influenced by this cycling process. Problems and images (goals) can approach unanimity. How these goals are accomplished creates controversy

(Stimson, 1991, p. 28). For example, crime control ranks near the top as something the government should take action on. The type of action to be taken, however, is in dispute. Some want more attention focused on punishment of convicted criminals while others focus their concern on crime prevention programs. Public support for solutions is subject to the ebb and flow of issue cycles while support for problems and goals remains stable.

How Can Individual Citizens and Groups Influence the Agenda?

The key to agenda influence is building a common demand about a problem and communicating that demand to those capable of responding with a solution. The first step in agenda building is recognizing a need, and forming an **opinion**, which means you become aware of a problem. The second step is to understand that someone shares your concern. This second step requires talking and listening to others (**deliberation**) in order to build a broader appeal for an issue. In the competition for a space on the collective agenda, not all issues have an equal chance of success. To plan strategies for agenda building, it is important to know which kinds of issues are more or less likely to succeed.

E.E. Schattschneider (1960) uses the term *redefinition* to refer to a process whereby support for an issue is gained by changing the lines of conflict to broaden the base of support. Baumgartner and Jones conclude, "Mobilization typically occurs through a redefinition of the prevailing policy image."(1993, p. 239) Expanding support and awareness for an issue depends in part on the characteristics of the issue. Cobb and Elder (1972) identify eight characteristics that improve the possibility of issue expansion to a larger public. In their view, an issue: should be broadly defined to appeal to various subgroups in the population, should be stated ambiguously in order to appeal broadly, should have clear social significance that can appeal to large social groups, should have long-term implications, should be defined nontechnically so it is easily understood, must be seen as new (without precedent), should be developed rapidly, and must have high emotional content. These characteristics are important because they provide guidelines for articulating issues in a way that will increase the probability of collective awareness.

How issues are framed or presented is an important strategic component of building an agenda. Studies of agenda building show that framing an issue in terms of the broadest possible common ground is the most effective way to move an issue on (or off) the agenda (Baumgartner and Jones, 1993 and Cobb and Elder, 1972). For an issue to get on the agenda, much less be acted on, there must be a common view that something needs to change. Eulau and Prewitt define the way people think about policy as consisting of problems, images, and solutions. Problems (or needs) are "the triggers for public policy" (1973, p. 524). Images are "guides to the future, what is to be achieved in a specific area" (1973, p. 534). Solutions are the "policy positions which link problems with images or goals" (1973, p. 540).

In framing issues for an agenda, it is important to identify problems or images, NOT solutions. Solutions tend to be technical, which leads to the dominance of experts over citizens. The debate over alternative solutions revolves around the efficiency of policy alternatives. Such a debate is likely to be resolved on its technical merits. Solutions also tend to be divisive—where people can agree on a problem or a goal they may still disagree on the optimal solution to the problem.

Problems and images are necessary elements if the issue is to achieve widespread support. The discussion of issues for inclusion on the agenda generally moves to link current problems with future expectations. For example, in many states the issue of educational financing draws considerable attention. The attention is often sparked by the view that property or sales taxes are too high (the problem) and should be lowered significantly (the image). Linking problems and images in the minds of a public is the first step an issue takes toward agenda status.

Building a citizen-based agenda is more difficult and time consuming than constructing an institutional agenda. Citizens will take longer to develop this common list of problems or goals because they need interaction to build consensus. In institutions, the interaction is not optional; it is routine. To build a citizen agenda, a mechanism for citizen interaction must be built up from scratch. A significant help in forming citizen agendas is that policy entrepreneurs are looking for slack resources that can be mobilized on behalf of an issue.

MECHANISMS

What are the mechanisms (rules) that translate individual concerns into public agenda items?

Agenda building requires three mechanisms:
- one to convert citizen opinion into action;

- one to expand the audience for an issue; and
- one to act on an issue.

Translating opinion to action requires organization. Organization of opinion is the function of interest groups, social movements, and political parties. The common element in movements, groups, and parties is that each of these mechanisms (in different ways) brings people together based on their shared goals and produces political action. Groups are advocates for private advantage through public policy. The Health Insurance Association of America lobbies for reimbursement and regulatory policies that will maximize the income of insurance companies in the organization. In many cases, the political participation of a group may only be a secondary reason for its existence. Movements take a common concern (such as racial justice) and mobilize organizations and citizens to take direct action to further their policy goal.

The political parties' goal is to win election by convincing voters that their candidates share the voters' concerns. Political parties identify with policy agendas in hopes of attracting voters. Black voters were brought into the Democratic party because of the party's commitment to placing the issue of civil rights on the national political agenda.

The media plays a central role in broadening the base of support for an issue (Lipsky, 1968). The creation of deliberative opportunities is critical as the media work to turn citizens into audiences instead of participants. Influencing the media to assist in the deliberative process of agenda building has become a crucial issue for democratic survival.

The media provide for a communication channel to a wider audience. The channel, however, has three important characteristics that make some messages more easily transmitted than others.

First, media outlets are businesses, which are expected to make a profit through large circulation of their product. The desire for viewers and readers affects which kinds of messages are carried. Conflict draws attention. This fact leads to media coverage of elections as a horse race between candidates. Candidates complain that media coverage comes only after the election, when it is too late to communicate their message.

Coverage of the president and Congress also tends to emphasize conflict and competition rather than cooperation. The identification of winners and losers simplifies complex processes and reduces the chances for constructive deliberation and compromise.

Second, since groups and experts debate solutions, members of the media also act as experts, preferring solutions to problems. Since the public is more likely to focus on problems, while the media and politicians focus on solutions, this debate is seen as irrelevant. Public deliberation is less dramatic and therefore underreported.

Third, coverage of an issue by media tends to follow groups or politicians who most actively utilize events to present issues. In the 1970s, for example, coverage of environmental issues tended to follow the lead of the most active environmental groups (Baumgartner and Jones, 1993, p. 106). The media build participatory democracy, where the voices of the active, the articulate, and those with assets (such as money and members) are amplified. Here the media encourages overt confrontation instead of thoughtful discussions. As a result of this process, some citizens are alienated from the political process because issues are not treated with the care they deserve.

Our federal system of shared powers between national, state, and local units of government offers opportunities for several institutions to become active in setting agendas. Mayors and city councils at the local level, governors and legislatures at the state level, the president and Congress at the national level, and courts at all three levels can assume a role in setting the agenda.

Policy images are closely linked to venues and policy types. For example, in the 1950s, nuclear power had a very positive image and was placed on the national agenda as a self-regulatory policy with the nuclear industry given substantial power. As doubts about the value and safety of nuclear power were raised in the 1970s and 1980s, state and national governments became more regulatory and took power away from the nuclear industry (Baumgartner and Jones, 1993, pp. 59-60).

The primary factor in determining the venue for moving an issue onto an agenda is the level of conflict. If there is consensus, then the agenda is set by policy networks or subgovernments. Executive agencies, legislative committees or subcommittees, and interest groups play a powerful role in setting the agenda when there is strong agreement on policy maps. When there is conflict, the dispute rises to the level of political leaders. Baumgartner and Jones summarize this connection, "Where the nature of the policy community changes from small, consensual, and homogeneous to large, conflictual, and heterogeneous, the likelihood increases that a given issue will rise higher on the national political agenda." (Baumgartner and Jones, 1993, p. 43) At the local level, agendas are dominated by business interest and the competition for economic development (Berry, 1993).

At all three levels, the executive branch has a large role in setting the agenda. The president dominates the national agenda.

The federal system increases the power of issue networks, which reach across political boundaries. The ability of those who have lost in one arena to place an issue on the agenda at another place or time is enhanced in a federal system (Anton, 1989, and Chesney, 1994).

TAKING ACTION

The core of the agenda building activity is the awareness by citizens and politicians of an issue. Awareness of an issue is built by recognizing **opinions**, building **knowledge**, communicating through a **deliberative** process, and **participation** in organizations that ratify and communicate issues to political leaders. Three activities are presented under agenda building:

1. building an agenda from experience
2. building an agenda from negotiation
3. building an agenda through telecommunications

The development of an agenda creates the opportunity for seeing relationships between components, thus allowing one to see the structure within which the issues emerge and the systematic responses that are required. These activities ask you to define and refine your opinions, deliberate with your classmates about your opinions, acquire knowledge about the issues that interest you and the rules that link you to other citizens, and finally to participate in the agenda structure designed by you and other citizens.

ACTIVITIES

ACTIVITY 2.1: Building an Agenda Face to Face

As a group, you and your classmates should share your views on which issues require immediate attention and how they relate to each other. Based on your different personal experiences in the urban environment, you will translate personal concerns into policy issues, deliberate on which of these issues should be on the collective agenda, and examine how these issues are related. In order to form a collective agenda you will exchange experiences, make strategic decisions on what you want to push, mobilize support for high-priority items, and try to make the agenda understandable to others. These activities cultivate an awareness of political issues and an appreciation for the rules by which political disputes are resolved.

The steps to setting up a collective agenda are:

STEP 1. Start with each of you presenting *one* issue to the class by stating why this issue is important to you, why it is important to the class, and why it should be included on the Urban Agenda. The class/group then votes to form study groups on the most important issues raised. Issue groups are formed if students are willing to participate.

STEP 2: Each issue group discusses how they feel and what they know about their issue. If necessary, members are dispatched to conduct additional research. Finally, the issue group writes a statement about why the issue is important and presents it to the class for inclusion in the class agenda.

STEP 3: The class reconvenes to hear the reports of the issue groups. They discuss:

1. How these issues interrelate (for example, are they components of a larger problem?), and if they can be dealt with at one time or require action on several fronts (a systems solution),
2. The nature and dimensions of the problems and the priority (attention) that each problem should receive,
3. How to present the high priority issues in a statement that others can understand and accept.

STEP 4: the group examine agendas from other groups such as the American Assembly, National League of Cities, the U.S. Conference of Mayors, or the National Issues Forum. Compare agenda objectives, clarity of statement, comprehensiveness, and the process used to formulate the statement.

STEP 5: Write up and share the agenda with other classes. Agree to participate in Activity 2 below.

STEP 6: Write a short paper on what you have learned from this process.

ACTIVITY 2.2: Building an Agenda from Negotiation

The task here is to pool the issues developed in the face-to-face agenda process to formulate an issues agenda for a larger group. This process requires representative democracy. Negotiators must be selected. These negotiators will have to bargain for issues on the agenda and must return to their groups to garner support for the agenda they have worked out. The final step is a ratifying convention to approve the draft agenda. This activity is designed to:

1. teach skills in bargaining and negotiation;
2. allow communication with diverse viewpoints; and,
3. provide an experience in which students can understand and use procedural rules to resolve political conflicts.

The steps to accomplish this activity are:

STEP 1: Receive the agendas from the face-to-face groups. Establish the ground rules for the negotiation process and the convention, including rules for who may vote, speak, and present amendments at the convention. The negotiation rules must address the following issues:

1. Which caucuses (face-to-face groups) are included in the negotiation?
2. How many votes does each caucus get? (Our negotiations have been based on one vote for each ten students.)
3. How many representatives may attend from each caucus?
4. Do the negotiators have the power to approve the draft agenda or must it be submitted to each caucus for a vote before it is approved as a draft for the convention?

STEP 2: Negotiators meet and identify the issues to be presented to the convention. Negotiators also finalize the convention rules. The rules used at a recent Urban Agenda Convention are:

1. The draft of the Urban Agenda Resolution must be moved and seconded by six caucuses (with a majority vote in each caucus) to be placed on the floor.
2. Once moved to the floor, each major issue will be discussed (90 seconds for and 90 seconds against) and then voted on. Speakers should line up behind floor microphones to be

recognized. To remain on the agenda, an issue must receive a majority vote of those at the convention.

3. Once the draft issues have been considered, the group will consider new issues and amendments to the Urban Agenda Resolution. Each new issue or amendment must have majority support in six sections to be moved to the convention floor. Each issue and amendment that is properly moved and seconded will be discussed (90 seconds for and 90 seconds against) and then voted on. A majority of those present and voting is required to pass the motion.

4. Voting will be by voice vote. If the chair cannot determine the majority on a voice vote, she or he will call for a show of hands. A majority of those present can request a poll of the caucuses to determine the actual vote.

5. Procedural points of order may be raised from the floor. A motion to adjourn has precedence over other motions. Quorum calls are not in order since those present and voting constitute a quorum for action.

Drafting committees are formed to develop statements on the high-priority issues identified earlier.

STEP 3: Negotiators return to their constituency and present the preliminary draft agenda. After discussion the negotiators may be asked to revise the draft.

STEP 4: Negotiators meet again and draft the final proposed Urban Agenda.

STEP 5: The Urban Agenda Convention is convened.

Two aspects of the convention deserve further discussion: the morning issue workshops and the afternoon caucuses. The morning workshops are designed to allow you to discuss policy topics that interest you. One suggested agenda for the discussion is: everyone introduces themselves; the draft statement in the area is reviewed (if there isn't one it can be drafted); problems are discussed; future activities related to the topic are suggested and discussed; and if action by the Urban Agenda Convention is necessary, strategies and tactics are discussed and implemented. A work group could become a coordinating committee to bring about changes to the Urban Agenda resolution in the afternoon session.

MODEL URBAN AGENDA CONVENTION PROGRAM

9-10 AM	OPENING SESSION Welcome Explanation of the convention (for guests) Rules of the convention (as drafted by the negotiators) Presentation of the draft agenda and *brief* statements of support by local leaders
10-12 AM	ISSUE WORKSHOPS You will organize simultaneous workshops on urban agenda issues, subissues, and activities. Examples of past workshops include: children at risk, violence, health care, crime, multicultural education, urban business development, social welfare, and substance abuse.
12-1 PM	LUNCH
1–3 PM	CAUCUSES You will meet in your face-to-face discussion groups to plan voting strategies for the floor of the convention, make final revisions in the draft urban agenda, and lobby for specific issues that may have been ignored previously.
3-4:30 PM	CLOSING SESSION Rules are explained again; agenda items are moved and seconded; items are debated; and a final vote is taken. Your caucuses will be negotiating prior to reconvening. Therefore, it is imperative that the order of rules be followed. Once the agenda is approved, there are speeches by national, state, and local elected officials you have invited to attend. In their speeches, the officials accept the agenda and promise to bring it to the attention of other elected officials and government bodies. The convention stands in adjournment until called together by another group of students and faculty.

The afternoon caucus sessions are where the politics of the convention are most visible. Each caucus must decide its priorities (which resolutions to accept and which issues to promote), negotiate with other caucuses, and determine its own style of operation. Caucus chair and caucus reporters (in case floor votes by caucuses are necessary) should be elected. You will have to send advocates for caucus positions to other caucuses to gather needed support. This is a critical part of the convention because it allows you to participate in the political bargaining process first hand and observe how people build political power.

Appendix A contains the Urban Agenda Convention Program and the Urban Agenda Resolution from April 9, 1994.

STEP 6: Participants evaluate the convention. Each caucus meets in class after the convention to discuss student reaction and views on the convention. Surveys handed out before and after the convention are completed by the participants. Appendix B contains the results of a poll of students who participated in the 1994 Urban Agenda Convention. As usual, you write a short paper on what they learned from this experience.

The time table for an Urban Agenda Convention fits into your thirteen-week semester:

Week 1	On the first day of class the professor introduces the project and sets the date for the Urban Agenda Convention.
Week 4	Begin face-to-face negotiations.
Week 7	Conclude face-to-face negotiations.
Week 8	Convene negotiators.
Week 10	Conclude negotiations and circulate draft resolutions to all caucuses.
Week 11	Hold Urban Agenda Convention. (Saturday works well because everyone can attend.)

ACTIVITY 2.3: Building an Agenda Using Telecommunications

The Urban Agenda Convention is ideal for learning how to use the electronic media. Developing skills in the electronic media is essential for operating in modern society. For example, issues such as how people allow meaningful discussions and differences of opinion to emerge and be dealt with in the context of media time and other restraints may be discussed. You can use the one-hour opening of the convention to discuss procedures and rules. You may also use guest speakers from community organizations and governmental institutions to provide an initial symbolic coalition. The closing session (voting the resolution, dealing with differences of opinion, providing for action commitments) teaches you how to deal with external structures and to confront the key problems of democracy in an environment of limited resources imposed by telecommunications costs.

STEP 1: Identify a group that will do the teleconference and have them check out potential resources: video capacity, cable, ITFS, public television. Many educational institutions have media centers that can produce this type of an event and can provide the technical advice necessary for planning a teleconference.

STEP 2: Ask your professor to contact faculty members at other schools who might be interested in doing the Urban Agenda Convention at their schools via teleconferencing.

STEP 3: Visit each potential site with your professor. Work out how they can use the teleconference for their own Urban Agenda Convention and how they will link up to your event. Delegations from other sites can vote on the final resolution by fax or phone and thereby be part of a convention without walls. If time permits, negotiators from schools in an area could convene to draft the agenda resolution.

STEP 4: After the convention, meet with faculty and other students to discuss their view of the process. You and the other students should fill out evaluation forms, which will quantify your opinions and lead to changes in future conventions.

CHAPTER 3

Community Coalitions and Coalition Building

While the building of the agenda involved individual and small group negotiation skills, the coalition building stage requires the identification of other groups with different, but potentially reconcilable, agendas. The essence of agenda building is: "If I am not for myself, who will be?" The essence of coalition building is: "If I am but for myself, what am I?"

Coalition building becomes necessary when one group's demands are not supported by sufficient power to force a desired response. Only partners who will support each other's demands can accumulate enough political power to obtain a response. If the response of a coalition partner is positive, then a coalition agenda and strategy must be developed. A new agenda emerging from this process must be acceptable to the partners and to the rank-and-file members who supported the initial agenda. For such a coalition to succeed, the partners must be capable of being both for themselves and for others.

While agenda building is designed to clarify needs and ultimately formulate the demands of a given group, coalition building requires the identification of potential agenda partners. Partners are individuals or groups who have different, but reconcilable, agendas. Partnerships are necessary if the agenda is to be responded to by policy makers. Coalition building demands that you express your views, listen to others' views, and find the common ground that unites you. Strategically, you may have to decide whether an issue is more or less important than gaining support for the agenda as a whole.

This chapter begins with a discussion of coalitions and coalition building. We discuss the role of advocacy, bargaining, and compromise in the development of coalitions.

Coalition building requires a continuous consciousnes of a potential partner's needs, experiences, styles of communication, and style of action. Coalition building depends on listening to others, expressing your own view, and finding the common ground that can unite you. In the heat of this process, it is easy to forget that the identification of common ground by one of the parties does not mean that common ground has been mutually found. Finding common ground and developing a common action strategy requires prioritizing issues and strategies from several groups simultaneously. A combination of advocacy, bargaining, compromise, communication, and analysis skills is critical for this process to work. Coalition partners need to remember that they joined together because they could not obtain a reasonable response to their demand alone.

The identification of potential agenda coalition partners is based on the majority rule principle of democracy, namely that, while decisions are made on the basis of majority votes, all majorities in a democracy are based on coalitions and are not permanent. In a situation where a majority decision results in the minority leaving, both are weakened politically.

Moving the governmental policy-making process requires agreement on both sides regarding which concerns are to be addressed and how pressure is to be applied to the government. The implementation of an action plan, such as a voter registration drive, a protest, boycott, or candidate endorsement increases the probability that the coalition's demands will gain a response. Without an action plan, demands can easily be ignored.

The first sign of a coalition is at the opening session of the Urban Agenda Convention. The students, through their contacts and those individuals they invited to the Agenda Convention already started the coalition building process. The guests invited to speak at the opening session represent possible coalition partners.

The outcome of building an agenda coalition is a broader base of support for the issues raised by you at the agenda convention. Successfully placing an issue on political and governmental agendas requires broad heterogeneous support. Building such support requires a carefully conceived coalition strategy.

The process of coalition building can be broken down into the four elements of civic literacy: opinions, knowledge, deliberation, and participation.

STAGE 1: OPINION

Identification of potential partners. At this stage, two principles are important: one is to start with the contacts represented at the agenda convention. Students and their guests are members of a wide variety of organizations, some of which can be brought into an agenda coalition. The second principle is that the search for coalition partners should be widespread. Such a search must include "nonpolitical" organizations. Olson and others have commented on the fact that many organizations have a primary goal that is not political even though they are active in the political process (unions and churches) (Olson, 1965). These groups should be courted to determine their interest in the coalition agenda. Special attention must be paid to organizations with political resources such as money or large memberships.

STAGE 2: KNOWLEDGE

Determine values and priorities of potential partners. Once partners and new constituencies are identified, attention shifts to understanding the priorities and values of potential coalition members. How do groups feel about the issues raised in the agenda statement? Is the constituency positive, neutral, or negative toward each issue raised? Most importantly, are there issues, which were not on the agenda that are important to the group?

These questions can only be answered by first systematically surveying each group. Based on interviews, each group's rating of the agenda issues is established. Ratings of additional issues are also obtained. The primary objective here is comprehensiveness, both in terms of the number of groups interviewed and in terms of the number of issues investigated. The information gathered at this stage must be summarized in a format that can be understood by all participants in the agenda coalition.

STAGE 3: DELIBERATION

Set up a negotiation process, identify spokespeople, and talk. Building an agenda coalition requires an inclusive process where there are no winners or losers. In popular terms, the negotiation must represent a win/win situation. In terms of game theory, the game must be nonzero sum in that a win for one group is not a loss for any other group (Gustafuson, Cats-Baril, and Alemi, 1992).

The identification of spokespersons is critical to the success of the project. These people must be able to articulate their constituency's point of view and must be able to listen to, and understand, other people's arguments. The primary task of a negotiator is to reach an agreement that can be sold to their constituencies.

STAGE 4: PARTICIPATION

Amend the agenda to reflect agreements and build commitment to an action plan. The value of formalizing agreements is that all parties to the agreement have an opportunity to articulate support for the negotiators' agreement. An agenda without any political action will not receive serious consideration by a political system that rewards power. Therefore, building political power for the agenda is necessary if the agenda is to be taken seriously.

You and your partners must move from participation in the internal negotiation process to participation in the wider political structures of national, state, and local governmental systems. Voter mobilization or protests or boycotts are actions that demonstrate political power and a resolve to be heard (Lipsky, 1968).

The centerpiece of the coalition building activity is a Coalition Inclusion Convention where the agenda from the activities presented in Chapter 2 is amended to include the agenda of coalition partners. Meetings with potential coalition partners will be organized and scheduled. During this phase of the process, students continue agenda issue research begun in relation to Chapter 2. Such research is focused on what the dimensions of the issue are and why they need to be addressed. Advocacy of these issues will also be required to convince coalition partners that it is an important concern. The Coalition Inclusion Convention should end with a commitment to action. Specifically, participants should agree to conduct a voter education/registration/mobilization campaign as the final act of the convention.

ACTIVITIES

ACTIVITY 3.1: Finding Coalition Partners

The coalition effort can take two routes: one is through your friends and relatives and the other is through your formal contacts with private and public organizations. One method is to poll elected officials and community group leaders to gauge their reaction and support for the Urban Agenda issues. By polling potential partners and identifying priorities and differences within the coalition, you will learn useful information and important political science skills.

STEP 1: At the Urban Agenda Convention, cards are distributed that ask students and guests for the names of any organization or institution that might be interested in being a member of the Urban Agenda Coalition and would go through a similar process of developing its own agenda.

STEP 2: A group of students reviews the cards gathered at the convention and develops a list of groups to contact and those participants willing to make the contacts.

STEP 3: A survey form on urban agenda issues is developed and sent to organizations and institutions identified in Step 2. The results of the survey are tabulated and analyzed.

STEP 4: Based on the analysis, you contact certain groups and ask them to endorse the Urban Agenda and action plans endorsed by the convention.

STEP 5: Small group discussions are held among the students to analyze both the group responses and the other students' reactions. Write a brief paper summarizing what you learned through this activity.

ACTIVITY 3.2: Building a Coalition: Agreeing on Strategies and Tactics

Having identified potential coalition partners, you must now discuss and implement a strategy for building a coalition. Three levels should be established (top leaders, organizational cadres, and rank-and-file members). You will need to establish a division of labor and a system of communication. During this activity you will learn how to sell the Urban Agenda and how to mobilize groups to participate in politics.

STEP 1: Using the information gathered in Activity 4, action plans are developed with specific groups. Planned actions may include in-depth policy studies, voter education programs, and outreach activities in other educational institutions.

STEP 2: The strategy and action plans are shared with other groups interested in the Urban Agenda. You should develop your own action plans and share these with other groups. Partners engage in their own activities and cooperate by working in their own areas on interrelated activities. You should avoid large, common superstructures or coordinating committees in favor of action-oriented meetings and activities. Each joint activity group is responsible for collecting data and sharing information on how well the activity worked.

STEP 3: You should analyze the data collected in Step 2 and decide the effectiveness of the activity evaluated. You will then report back to the other students and partners involved in the project.

ACTIVITY 3.3: Bringing Elected Officials and Units of Local Government into the Coalition

Since governmental institutions set policy agendas, strategies to bring these entities into the agenda coalition are essential. Although these entities are not private groups, the mechanisms used to include them in the agenda process is identical to the process used for other groups. As with other coalition partners, the first step is to understand their priorities and problems and to inform them about the content of the current agenda.

STEP 1: Determine how sympathetic officials and units of government are to the issues raised at the Agenda Convention. There are two ways this can be done. One is simply to survey (by mail, phone, or preferably in person) officials in each unit of government. A more intensive method is to form study groups made up of local officials, faculty, and students, which meet and consider the issues raised by the Agenda Convention. Each study group should write their own issues statement to be shared in a meeting with all of the other study groups. The result of this process is a resolution to which all of the groups agree.

STEP 2: This is the endorsement and communication phase. During this phase, elected officials ask their institutions (for example city council, county commission, or school board) for a resolution endorsing the positions taken by the Agenda Convention and/or the study groups. An example of this kind of activity is the model resolution endorsing the Urban Agenda Convention in Detroit, which follows on page 105. These resolutions are then circulated to the media and other interested parties.

MODEL RESOLUTION IN SUPPORT OF URBAN AGENDA:
1996 RESOLUTION NO._____

WHEREAS, the National League of Cities' *Invest in Hometown American Agenda* was established to inform and educate the Presidential candidates on issues of importance and concerns to the nation's cities, and

WHEREAS, this Agenda outlines the needs of urban America and emphasizes the interrelationships between our nation's urban centers and their suburbs and rural areas, and

WHEREAS, the Politicial Science Department of Wayne State University is sponsoring an *Urban Agenda: 1996* in cooperation with the National League of Cities' *Invest in Hometown America Agenda*, and

WHEREAS, Wayne State University has held several citizen's conventions in past months for the purpose of Voter Registration and Education and addressing further issues facing the nation's cities, and

WHERAS, the *Urban Agenda: 1996 Project* has invited the Presidential candidates to appear in Detroit prior to the 1996 presidential election, to be interviewed on their views regarding issues of importance to the Urban Agenda,

NOW, THEREFORE BE IT RESOLVED, that _____ does hereby adopt and recommend the *Urban Agenda: 1996* to all candidates for the Office of the Presidency, and

BE IT FURTHER RESOLVED, that the _____ does hereby urge the Presidential candidates to come to Detroit in the Fall of 1996 to address this Urban Agenda and discuss their qualifications for the Presidency, and

BE IT FURTHER RESOLVED, that a copy of this resolution be forwarded to each Presidential campaign, and to.W.S.U.'s Department of Political Science.

STEP 3: This involves the implementation of projects through joint action. Three types of projects are: internships, issues forums, and joint voter participation programs. Local governments, school boards, and elected officials can offer internships to students to analyze issues related to the agenda, including voter participation and evaluation of city and county services. Communication students, working with local officials and local cable companies, can offer talk shows on agenda issues or issues related to local education and government. These shows can be used in high school and university civics courses. Many of the activities outlined in the next several chapters on voter participation can be implemented by joint committees made up of students, coalition partners, and public officials.

CHAPTER 4

Voter Registration and Identification

One of the best examples of how governments make decisions, irrespective of who participates, is in elections. Elections are held routinely with winners determined by which candidate receives the most votes. The election decision stands whether the voter turnout is 30 percent or 90 percent. The Republican and Democratic Parties in 1996 nominated Senator Dole and President Clinton as presidential candidates based on primary elections where turnout was less than ten percent. Even if only half of the population is eligible to vote, the results will be certified and a winner declared. The voices of those excluded from voting are not considered. **There is no vacuum**; candidates will run for office and be elected with or without your participation.

Where large groups are excluded from voting there is a political opportunity. Electoral participation is a political resource. If a group can be made eligible to vote and mobilized to the polls, the distribution of power in the political system can be altered and new demands acted upon. Groups and individuals in power will try to retain their advantage by mobilizing supporters. Your job is to mobilize your supporters to political participation by getting them registered to vote. Building political power through elections requires you to push your way into the political process.

The skills of civic literacy are crucial for registering new voters. Voter registration focuses on thought and action within a political structure. **Knowledge** of voter registration laws is vital for planning an effective strategy for voter registration campaigns. The logistics of a voter registration drive are determined by rules established by your local officials. Issues such as where to get registration forms, where and when to turn the forms in, and where potential voters can be contacted are established by voter registration rules.

Citizen **opinions** on civic duty and **deliberations** on the importance of political decisions and voter registration are important steps leading to more structured political activity. People will register when they understand that the government is making decisions that affect them directly. For example, lower rates of urban voter registration can be countered by showing urban residents how programs helping urban areas are being cut because they choose not to participate in the voting process.

The core of voter registration is simply asking someone to register as a voter. This one-on-one citizen interaction is at the center of all political **participation**. It can be accomplished through an organized voter registration drive or by someone acting alone, simply asking people if they are registered. In either case the political act is one of direct citizen interaction.

To conduct a voter registration drive, you need: a **desire** or motivation to engage in this activity based on your opinions and resources; a **plan** based on knowledge of the laws and rules in your state; and an **active cadre** of citizens who can implement the plan by asking people to register to vote. Building a plan and an active cadre requires deliberation on both the political issues, which provide motivation, and the feasibility of the planned registration drive.

Because political structure is so important for this activity, we begin with a discussion of voter registration and ballot access rules. The activity section presents the step-by-step mechanics for organizing a voter registration drive. At the end of the chapter we discuss individual factors, such as opinions and resources that influence participation.

VOTER REGISTRATION RULES

If you want to vote in an election, you must be registered (except in North Dakota). This simple fact has not always been true in the U.S., is not true in most western democracies, and is a barrier that keeps citizens from voting. These facts illustrate the point that to participate in politics at any level you have to understand the structure you are working within. You can't help people vote if you don't know how to get them registered.

This chapter focuses on thought and action within a political structure. We discuss knowledge concerning rules governing who can vote, what impact these rules have on participation, and how these rules can be used to establish voter registration activities.

Of the world's major democracies, only France, New Zealand, Australia, and the U.S. do not have automatic voter registration (Powell, 1986). Some democracies do more than encourage voting—they require it. Fines and other penalties are imposed on citizens who do not vote in Greece, Italy and Belgium. Voter turnout is especially high (94 percent) in Italy, which has both automatic registration and penalties for not voting (Powell, 1986).

The introduction of voter registration laws in the U.S. was designed to limit voting to qualified citizens and to reduce cases of multiple voting. However good the intentions, voter registration laws have reduced election turnout. Burns, Pelteson, Cronin, and Magelby point out that turnout declined from the 80 percent range to 50 percent range with the introduction of these "reforms" (Burns, Pelteson, Cronin, and Magelby, 1993, p. 328).

Raymond Wolfinger and Steven Rosenstone calculate that if registration laws were more lenient (for example by extending registration to election day, or allowing registration in shopping malls), turnout would increase 9 percent. The greatest barriers to voting are: early closing dates for registration, irregular office hours, no Saturday or Sunday registration, and no absentee registration (Wolfinger and Rosenstone, 1980, p. 88).

Not surprisingly, states such as North Dakota, Maine and Oregon, which have the least restrictive voter registration laws also boast the highest turnout rates, while states in the South with the most restrictive laws have the lowest turnout (Gray, Jacob, and Albritton, 1990, Table 3.1).

The most graphic example of voter registration as a barrier to voting was in the South before 1964. The 1965 Voting Rights Law sent federal officials into counties where literacy tests were used and where less than 50 percent of the eligible voters were registered. The impact of this effort was dramatic. From 1960–1968 the registration of black voters rose significantly in southern states. Table 4.1 on page 40 summarizes changes in voter registration in the South.

In Georgia, white registration increased faster than black registration. President Carter's description of Georgia politics during this period demonstrates that voter registration laws and the county unit

TABLE 4.1 Change in Black and White Voter Registration in Southern States Before and After the 1965 Voting Rights Act

	CHANGE IN THE PERCENT OF VOTERS REGISTERED BETWEEN 1960 AND 1968	
	Black	White
Alabama	37.9	26.0
Arkansas	24.8	12.4
Florida	24.0	12.1
Georgia	23.3	23.5
Louisiana	27.8	16.2
Mississippi	54.8	27.6
North Carolina	12.2	-9.1
South Carolina	37.5	24.6
Tennessee	12.6	7.6
Texas	26.1	10.8
Virginia	32.5	17.3

SOURCE: Calculated from Herbert B. Asher, *Presidential Elections and American Politics,* 4th Ed., Chicago, IL: Dorsey Press. Table 2.3.

method of allocating votes were constructed to dilute the votes of blacks and urban dwellers (Carter, 1992, p. xxii and pp. 23–25). The removal of voting registration barriers, combined with the 1962 Supreme Court decision in *Baker* v. *Carr,* which stipulated that all votes had to count equally, increased the participation and power of previously disenfranchised groups of citizens.

Even though large numbers of citizens were disenfranchised, the political system had no trouble making decisions and carrying out policy. In fact, the system was self-sustaining and quite resistant to change. In the case of Georgia, only pressure from outside combined with mobilization of new political constituencies produced political reform. The rise of black elected officials and moderate Southern white politicians, such as Presidents Carter and Clinton, illustrate the political consequences of removing obstacles to citizen participation.

The most recent attempt to increase voter participation is passage of the Motor Voter Bill. The National Voter Registration Act of 1993, the "Motor Voter Law" (P.L 103-31), seeks to increase the number of citizens who register to vote in federal elections by:

1. Allowing citizens to register in three ways: by mail, in person, or when applying for a driver's license or public assistance.
2. Preventing election officials from taking voters off the registration lists simply for failure to vote.

3. Requiring a program for positively confirming the accuracy of registration information in a uniform and nondiscriminatory manner.
4. Providing a "fail-safe" procedure whereby voters will be allowed to vote despite legal, bureaucratic, or clerical problems.

The net effect of this law is to move the burden of registration from the voters to the government. Election officials are now responsible for reaching out to voters to register and to monitor changes in residence or voting status.

The Motor Voter Bill only applies to federal elections and must have been implemented before January 1995 (January 1996 if the state constitution must be amended). In the U.S. federal system, states are primarily responsible for establishing laws regarding the organization, timing, financing, and qualifications for elections. Therefore, implementation of this law is up to state legislatures and state election officials.

Most states amended their election laws to comply with the Motor Voter Law. Key features of state laws in effect when President Clinton signed the Motor Voter Bill into law are summarized in Tables 4.2 on page 42 and 4.3 on page 43. North Dakota, which does not require registration, is exempt. Only four states had both driver's license and welfare office registration procedures and twenty states had neither type of registration. Twenty-two states did not have provisions for mail registration. Only eleven states do not purge voter lists. States will need information-processing capabilities to share information on changes in voter status (such as moving or dying) with federal agencies such as the U.S. Postal Service and local jurisdictions responsible for keeping voter lists.

In Michigan, the National Voter Registration Act allows citizens to register by mail, at federal and state offices, or in person at the county, city, or township clerk's office. Citizens may help others to register or update their address by handing out and collecting mail-in forms and delivering these forms to the local election official (in Michigan this includes city, township, or county clerks).

Not all of the changes in Michigan's implementation of the National Motor Voter Bill in Michigan are positive. The Deputy Voter Registrar program, which trained people to accept voter applications directly, has been eliminated. This program was used by Michigan County Clerks and voluntary organizations to promote registration of voters by unpaid volunteers.

TABLE 4.2 Summary of State Registration Laws at the Time President Clinton Signed the National Voter Registration Act, May 20, 1993

State	Deadline for Registration	Mail Registration	Registration Canceled Automatically
Alabama	10 days	no	no
Alaska	30 days	yes-notary	yes, 2 years
Arizona	29 days	no	yes, 1 election
Arkansas	20 days	yes	yes, 4 years
California	29 days	yes	no
Colorado	25 days	no	yes, 2 elections
Connecticut	21 days	yes-witness	no
Delaware	11 days	yes-2 step	yes, 4 years
D.C.	30 days	yes	no
Florida	30 days	no	yes, 2 years
Georgia	30 days	no	yes, 3 years
Hawaii	30 days	yes	yes, 2 elections
Idaho	10 days	no	yes, 4 years
Illinois	28 days	no	yes, 4 years
Indiana	29 days	yes	yes, 4 years
Iowa	10 days	yes	yes, 2 years
Kansas	14 days	yes-2 step	yes, 2 elections
Kentucky	28 days	yes	no
Louisiana	24 days	no	no
Maine	0 days	yes	no
Maryland	29 days	yes	yes, 5 years
Massachusetts	28 days	no	no
Michigan	30 days	no	yes, 5 years
Minnesota	0 days	yes	yes, 4 years
Mississippi	30 days	yes-witness	yes, 4 years
Missouri	20 days	no	no
Montana	30 days	yes-notary	yes, 1 pres. elec
Nebraska	18 days	yes-witness	no
Nevada	30 days	yes	yes, 1 election
New Hampshire	10 days	no	yes, 3 elections
New Jersey	29 days	yes-witness	yes, 4 years
New Mexico	28 days	no	yes, 8 years
New York	25 days	yes	yes, 2 elections
North Carolina	21 days	no	yes, 2 pres.elec
North Dakota	no registration required		
Ohio	30 days	yes	yes, 4 years
Oklahoma	10 days	no	yes, 8 years
Oregon	20 days	yes	yes, 2 elections
Pennsylvania	30 days	yes	yes, 2 years
Rhode Island	30 days	no	yes, 5 years
South Carolina	30 days	yes-witness	yes, 2 elections
South Dakota	15 days	no	yes, 4 years
Tennessee	30 days	yes-notary	yes, 4 years
Texas	30 days	yes	no
Utah	5 days	yes	yes, 4 years
Vermont	17 days	yes	yes, 4 years

TABLE 4.2 *Continued*

State	Deadline for Registration	Mail Registration	Registration Canceled Automatically
Virginia	30 days	no	yes, 4 years
Washington	30 days	no	yes, 4 years
West Virginia	30 days	yes-notary	yes, 2 elections
Wisconsin	0 days	yes-witness	yes, 4 years
Wyoming	30 days	no	yes, 1 election

Sources:

Implementation Manual for the National Voter Registration Act. 1993. New York: Human SERVE.

Implementing the National Voter Registration Act of 1993: Requirements, Issues, Approaches, and Examples. 1993. Washington, DC: The Federal Election Commission.

Personal Communication from Joanne Chasnow, Associate Director of Human SERVE's 100% Vote Campaign for Universal Voter Registration, to James Chesney, March, 1994.

VOTE! The First Steps. 1988. Washington, DC:League of Women Voters of the United States.

VOTE! The First Steps: Supplemental Update 1992. 1992. Washington, DC:League of Women Voters of the United States.

TABLE 4.3 Summary of State Motor Voter and Agency-Based Voter Registration Laws at the Time President Clinton Signed the National Voter Registration Act, May 20, 1993

	MOTOR VOTER	AGENCY-BASED		
State	Combined License and Registration System	Forms Available License	Agency	Mandatory Question
Alabama	no	no	no	no
Alaska	no	yes	no	no
Arizona	yes	no	no	no
Arkansas	no	no	yes	no
California	no	no	no	no
Colorado	no	no	no	no
Connecticut	yes	yes	yes	no
Delaware	no	no	no	no
D.C.	yes	no	no	no
Florida	no	no	no	no
Georgia	no	no	no	no
Hawaii	yes	no	yes	no
Idaho	no	no	no	no
Illinois	no	yes	no	no
Indiana	no	no	no	no
Iowa	yes	no	yes	no
Kansas	yes	no	no	no
Kentucky	no	no	no	no

Continued

TABLE 4.3 *Continued*

State	MOTOR VOTER Combined License and Registration System	AGENCY-BASED Forms Available License	Agency	Mandatory Question
Louisiana	no	yes	no	no
Maine	no	no	no	no
Maryland	no	yes	yes	no
Massachusetts	no	no	no	no
Michigan	yes	no	no	no
Minnesota	yes	no	no	yes
Mississippi	yes	no	no	no
Missouri	no	no	no	no
Montana	yes	no	no	no
Nebraska	no	no	no	no
Nevada	yes	no	no	no
New Hampshire	no	no	no	no
New Jersey	no	no	yes	no
New Mexico	no	yes	no	no
New York	yes	no	yes	yes
North Carolina	yes	no	no	no
North Dakota	no registration required			
Ohio	yes	no	yes	no
Oklahoma	no	yes	yes	no
Oregon	yes	no	no	no
Pennsylvania	no	yes	no	yes
Rhode Island	no	yes	yes	no
South Carolina	no	no	no	no
South Dakota	no	no	no	no
Tennessee	no	yes	no	no
Texas	yes	no	no	no
Utah	no	no	no	no
Vermont	no	yes	no	no
Virginia	no	no	no	no
Washington	yes	no	yes	no
West Virginia	yes	no	no	no
Wisconsin	no	no	no	no
Wyoming	no	no	no	no

Sources:

Implementing the National Voter Registration Act of 1993: Requirements, Issues, Approaches, and Examples. 1993. Washington, DC: The Federal Election Commission.

Implementation Manual for the National Voter Registration Act. 1993. New York: Human SERVE

Personal Communication from Joanne Chasnow, Associate Director of Human SERVE's 100% Vote Campaign for Universal Voter Registration, to James Chesney, March, 1994.

VOTE! The First Steps. 1988. Washington, DC: League of Women Voters of The United States.

VOTE! The First Steps: Supplemental Update 1992. 1992. Washington, DC: League of Women Voters of The United States.

Mail-in forms are available and can be collected and handed in to the clerk's office by anyone. **HOWEVER**, citizens using the mail-in form to register or change voting jurisdictions MAY NOT **vote absentee** in the next election. This provision discourages some voters and makes registering voters more difficult.

In order to register voters and have them eligible for absentee ballots, county clerks must appoint election assistants and organizations must recruit people for this task. County, city, and township clerks may appoint election assistants under their own authority and pay for training out of their own budgets. To find out how your state is implementing the Moter Voter Law, contact your state election official whose name and address are listed in Appendix B.

The Moter Voter Law is having a positive impact on voter registration. Richard Cloward estimates that by 1996 20 million of the 65 million unregistered voters will have signed up to vote.(HumanSERVE Press Release, March 29,1995). Nearly 400,000 people were registered in the first three months of the program (Chasnow, 1995).

RULES ON BALLOT ACCESS

Once the obstacle of voter registration is cleared, access to the ballot becomes a central concern. Issues such as how long the polls are open, whether polling places are handicapped accessible, availability of absent ballots and the procedure for returning absent ballots, and the politeness and efficiency of poll workers all influence voter turnout. States seek to ensure ballot access by providing absentee ballots automatically to elderly or handicapped voters, braille ballots for blind voters, and curbside service for handicapped voters (Council of State Governments, 1980, p.54). Table 4.4 on page 46 summarizes state laws on ballot access. The logical extensions of many of these programs is the Texas early-voter system and Oregon's mail election.

Governor Ann Richards signed the Texas Early Voting Law on May 26, 1991. The law made five substantial changes to the Texas Election Law:

1. All references to **absent voting** were replaced with the words "**early voting**." This change in election law removed any restriction on who could vote before election day.
2. Early votes will be counted by precinct and polling place location. In most areas the absentee votes are counted by total jurisdiction (ie., city or township). Early votes will thus be combined with election day results to give precinct totals that cover all voters.

3. Counties are required to have early voting polling places open for specified times during the week and on the last weekend of early voting. Counties with more than 100,000 population must keep the main early vote polling place open at least twelve hours a day Monday through Friday, twelve hours on Saturday, and five hours on Sunday of the week before the election. Polling places for early voting will be open for nearly eighty hours during the week before the election. The main early voter polling place must also be open on election day.

4. In addition to the main early voter polling place, branch early voter polling places may/must be established. Requirements for the existence and location of branches are outlined in the law. The hours of operation are the same as outlined above for the main early voting polling place.

5. Voters who become ill or disabled shortly before the election may apply for a late voting ballot until 2PM of election day (Hanna, 1991).

TABLE 4.4 State Laws on Ballot Access and Absent Voters

State	Absent Voter Qualification	Application Deadline		Ballot Return Deadline
		Person	Mail	
Alabama	any absence	5 days	5 days	election day
Alaska	none	0 days	4 days	election day
Arizona	any absence	4 days	4 days	election day
Arkansas	any absence	1 day	1 day	1 day
California	none	7 days	7 days	election day
Colorado	any absence	4 days	4 days	election day
Connecticut	any absence	0 days		1 day
Delaware	any absence	1 day	3 days	1 day
D.C.	any absence	1 day	7 days	1 day
Florida	any absence	0 days	0 days	election day
Georgia	any absence	1 day	1 day	1 day
Hawaii	none	7 days	7 days	election day
Idaho	any absence	1 day	1 day	election day
Illinois	any absence	1 day	5 days	1 day
Indiana	any absence	0 days	5 days	election day
Iowa	any absence	0 days	1 day	election day
Kansas	none	1 day	1 day	election day
Kentucky	any absence	7 days	7 days	mail election
Louisiana	any absence	6 days	4 days	6 days
Maine	any absence	0 days	0 days	election day
Maryland	some absences	7 days	7 days	election day

TABLE 4.4 *Continued*

State	Absent Voter Qualification	Application Deadline Person	Mail	Ballot Return Deadline
Massachusetts	some absences	1 day	1 day	1 day
Michigan	any absence	1 day	4 days	election day
Minnesota	any absence	1 day	1 day	election day
Mississippi	some absences	4 days	vague	election day
Missouri	any absence	1 day	6 days	1 day
Montana	any absence	1 day	1 day	1 day
Nebraska	any absence	1 day	5 days	election day
Nevada	any absence	7 days	7 days	election day
New Hampshire	any absence	0 days	0 days	election day
New Jersey	any absence	1 day	7 days	election day
New Mexico	any absence	5 days	5 days	election day
New York	any absence	1 day	7 days	election day
North Carolina	any absence	5 days	7 days	1 day
North Dakota	none	1 day		1 day
Ohio	any absence	1 day	1 day	election day
Oklahoma	early voting	6 days	6 days	mail
Oregon	none	0 days	5 days	election day
Pennsylvania	any absence	7 days	7days	4 days
Rhode Island	some absences	21 days	21 days	election day
South Carolina	any absence	1 day	4 days	1 day
South Dakota	any absence	0 days	0 days	election day
Tennessee	any absence	5 days	7 days	election day
Texas	early voting			
Utah	any absence	1 day	4 days	election day
Vermont	any absence	1 day	1 day	election day
Virginia	valid reason	3 days	5 days	election day
Washington	none	1 day	1 day	election day
West Virginia	none	1 day	1 day	1 day
Wisconsin	any reason	1 day	4 days	1 day
Wyoming	none	0 days	0 days	election day

Sources:

Implementing The National Voter Registration Act of 1993: Requirements, Issues, Approaches, and Examples. 1993. Washington, DC: The Federal Election Commission.

Implementation Manual for the National Voter Registration Act. 1993. New York: Human SERVE

Personal Communication from Joanne Chasnow, Associate Director of Human SERVE's 100% Vote Campaign for Universal Voter Registration, to James Chesney, March, 1994.

VOTE! The First Steps. 1988. Washington, DC: League of Women Voters of The United States.

VOTE! The First Steps: Supplemental Update 1992. 1992. Washington, DC: League of Women Voters of The United States.

TURNOUT

The removal of ballot barriers, such as in the Texas Early Voting Law, does not automatically increase turnout. Only removing barriers *and* increasing the motivation of voters will improve turnout. Turnout figures are presented in Table 4.5 for elections before (1986 and 1988) and after (1990, 1992, and 1994) implementation of early voting in Texas. Early voting does not appear to increase turnout in low-visibility primary elections, but does improve turnout in higher visibility general elections. Table 4.5 shows turnout in presidential primaries is the same before and after the implementation of the early voting system.

General election turnout is greater after implementation of early voting for both president and governor. The increase in governors' races is roughly 3.5 percentage points. Turnout in the higher visibility presidential general election improved a substantial 10 percentage points from 1988 to 1992. The increase in presidential voting is due to several factors, such as the competitiveness of campaigns, the presence of two Texans (Bush and Perot) on the ballot in 1992, increases in turnout at the national level, and the early voting system. Twenty-five percent of the Texas voters vote early. The increased cost of the program is estimated to be 25 percent.

The emphasis on structure (knowledge and participation) should not obscure the importance of citizens (opinions and deliberation). The civic component of civic literacy consists of both citizens and structure. Individual characteristics are also important factors in understanding why people register and vote in elections. In order to

TABLE 4.5 Voter Turnout for Various Elections in Texas Before and After the Early Voting Law.

	1988	1990
Presidential Primary Election Turnout		
Republicans	10%	10%
Democrats	19%	18.6%
General Election Turnout		
Presidential	66.2%	72.9%

	1986	1990	1994
Gubernatorial	47.2	50.5	50.8

SOURCE: Texas Secretary of State, Election Division.

register voters, you need to understand these citizen characteristics and how they have changed in the recent past.

CITIZEN CHARACTERISTICS

Four citizen characteristics that influence voting participation are:

1. **Resources.** Numerous studies show that individuals with more money, education, and status are more likely to participate in elections. People without resources obviously have a more difficult time overcoming the barriers to participation (Conway, 1991; Rosenstone and Hansen, 1993; and Wolfinger and Rosenstone, 1980).

2. **Citizen Duty.** Some people believe they should participate in elections even if they don't care very much about the outcome. This belief is called citizen duty—the idea that one has a responsibility to participate irrespective of outcome. Since 1980 there has been a very substantial drop in citizen duty. In the 1980 National Election Study, 59 percent said they should vote even if they did not care about the election. By 1988, there had been a 17-point decline, as only 42 percent felt that way (Teixeira, 1992, p. 55).

3. **Political Efficacy.** The opinion that your vote counts and can make a difference is political efficacy. People who view their vote as important will take the trouble to exercise their franchise. The idea that government is responsive to voters also has declined sharply since 1960. In 1960, 61.7 percent reported that they felt the government was highly responsive; only 29.9 percent responded that way in 1988 (Teixeira, 1992, p. 44).

4. **Social and Political Networks.** Citizens who are part of social, political, or community organizations are more likely to participate in politics by voting. Being connected to other people in your community increases the availability of political information and the opportunity to discuss political topics. These opportunities have a positive impact on participation.

Civic literacy and voter registration are closely intertwined. If citizens are going to become registered voters and exercise their right to vote, opinions such as citizen duty and political efficacy must be combined with the opportunity to communicate provided by social networks. Taking action by talking to, and registering, voters can change these attitudes. At the structural level, well-planned voter registration drives not only improve participation rates, but they also can help build a connection to the political system. Therefore, voter registration activity *may* reverse recent declines in citizen duty and political efficacy.

VOTER REGISTRATION ACTIVITIES

Two activities are outlined.

ACTIVITY 4.1: Analysis and Change of State Voter Registration Laws

An analysis of the state's voter registration legislation and administration is conducted. This activity is necessary both in order to organize voter registration activities effectively and to recommend and advocate changes in election laws.

STEP 1: Obtain copies of your state's election law and voter registration information from state and local officials.

STEP 2: Discuss voter registration laws in class groups to determine which issues your think should be addressed in any voter registration law reform. You may want to begin with questions such as: What obstacles would you encounter in conducting a voter registration drive in your community? Are there any state laws that discourage this activity? Would voter registration drives be easier in other states? In which states would it be most difficult to conduct voter registration drives? Are there other groups or individuals who want these laws changed? Whose support would you need to conduct a voter registration drive? What barriers exist to conducting a voter registration drive in your community high schools? Whose support do you need for this activity? Would a voter registration drive change the politics in your community? Who would gain and lose power in the event of a successful registration effort?

STEP 3: Invite local and state election officials to present their views on election reform to your class or to a specially organized conference on the topic. Holding a conference on this topic will allow you to identify other groups interested in the issue and increase your visibility on this issue. As part of this activity, you and your classmates should write and circulate position papers on needed changes in state election laws and administration.

STEP 4: Hold a series of meetings with state legislators, state administrative officials, and interest group leaders to discuss the group's recommendations on voter registration law reform. Build support and strategies for legislative changes to voter registration laws. This effort may be more successful than you imagine. A lobbying effort for less restrictive registration and ballot access policies undertaken by our students in Michigan in 1989 successfully changed the voter registration law so that county clerks could train and empower deputy voter registrars.

ACTIVITY 4.2: Voter Registration Drives

Asking and helping someone to register to vote is a political activity that builds your awareness of the political process and of citizen opinions. Most people find this is much easier to do than they expect. The activity provides an easy first step into politics. It combines taking action (asking someone to register to vote) with information (knowing the requirements for registration). This activity involves a fundamental civic literacy skill.

STEP 1: The strategy for your voter registration drive is dependent on your state laws and regulations. Tables 4.2 and 4.3 summarize salient features. Since most states allow mail-in registration, you can plan a drive in which you and other students/volunteers hand out mail applications in a wide variety of locations.

STEP 2: Once you have an initial strategy for the voter registration drive, contact the state agency responsible for election administration. In most states, this is the secretary of state's office. A few states have independent election commissions. The election administration office can provide useful advice and information on specific components of the drive. Appendix B contains a list of the election officials for each state. The office will provide you with the name, address, and phone number of the local election official with whom you will want to work very closely. Our Civic Literacy Project has been fortunate to have strong support, help, and encouragement from Teola P. Hunter, Wayne County Clerk, and Wayne County Commissioner George Cushingberry.

STEP 3: One key strategic decision is the location for the drive. College campuses, high schools, shopping malls, union halls, and door-to-door on local streets are all good locations. High school drives in the spring are especially productive. You can organize teams of college students to go back to their former high school civics classes to register new voters. This venue offers the college students an opportunity to provide a service to their high schools, provides the high schools a vehicle for registering their students, and creates close ties between high schools, and universities. You must decide which of these alternatives is likely to be most productive.

STEP 4: Training is the most critical phase. Training must cover legal requirements for voting and registering voters, sample scripts, and reporting forms. The training is more extensive if your state allows registration by deputy voter registrars. An outline for learning how to do voter registration is presented as an aid to organizing these sessions.

Registration Training Outline

1. Discuss voter registration drive strategies and goals. How will the drive operate? Will students be deputized or accept mail-in registrations? Will other groups be working with student/volunteers? This is a good place to discuss the system for earning class points.
2. Think about and discuss your responsibilities. What tools and information do you need to accomplish your tasks? In Michigan, Deputy Voter Registrars are required, so our students are trained by the county clerk's office and sworn in as Deputy Voter Registrars. The training they receive as part of that process includes: who can be a deputy voter registrar, who is eligible to vote, how to fill out a voter application form, the difference between post office address and political jurisdictions, and limitations on where applications can be accepted (for example, they cannot be accepted in bars in Michigan). Although the form used in most states is simple, it must be filled out accurately and completely if the voter is going to be successfully registered.
3. Find or develop reporting forms needed to monitor progress toward the project's goals. Make sure you and your group know the schedule for the registration drive. Answer questions such as: How will time spent and number of voters registered be recorded? Where should my forms be taken?
4. Write and rehearse scripts on how potential voters can be approached and asked to register. Useful hints: Energy pays! (Don't just sit at the table; get up and bring people over to reg-

ister.) Ask questions positively and directly. (Are you registered to vote? If not, do you want to be a voter in the next election?) Work in high-traffic, high-visibility locations.

STEP 5: The drive is set in motion and monitored. You and your classmates divide into teams and choose locations. Organizing the logistics (having forms, flyers, permissions) is vital to the success of the drive. Thinking through what is needed for each situation, and getting it there, is vitally important. For example, make sure you have registration forms or the drive's effectiveness will be severely hampered.

STEP 6: Monitoring improves overall performance. You should choose a few people to review all completed voter registration applications for completeness before these forms are handed in to the election officials. Election officials are more cooperative when they know that they will receive valid and complete applications from a drive.

STEP 7: Have a celebration. Plan a big event to turn in voter applications and reward student workers for a job well done. The event should feature people who helped the drive and a well-known speaker. You will know that you have accomplished something important with the drive.

STEP 8: Hold candid discussions with other students, volunteers, and election officials to yield suggestions for the next drive. You need to schedule the following meetings at the conclusion of the voter registration drive:

1. student / volunteer discussion groups
2. visits to key contacts—county clerk, state election officials, and
3. forums with participating groups.

CHAPTER 5

Voter Education

As is the case with any civic literacy activity, voter education is not just a public good with broad and intangible rewards. It is an opportunity to explore needs, explain problems, and gather support for your issue agenda with both candidates and citizens. Voter education activities open channels of communication to promote your issues. If used properly, these channels can produce support for your agenda. To help you understand voter education, we discuss voter opinions, information, and action.

One of the most hotly debated topics in political science is over the question: how much information do voters have (or need) to make a decision on election day. The state of civic knowledge is generally regarded as low. Few voters know their congressperson's name, much less his or her position on crucial issues of the day. Voters need information upon which they can base action (vote).

The debate in political science over how much or how little information voters have misses the essential point that information is ALWAYS limited and decisions are made anyway. No one has a complete and comprehensive picture of government activity on every issue. Instead, voters make decisions with the information available to them when they enter the voting booth. Which issues they think are important and what information they have is a function of who participates in the election campaign. The connection between voting and thinking is summarized by Samuel Popkin, "Voters consider only the few issues they can connect with particular offices and with results they care about." (Popkin, 1991, p. 97)

Election campaigns play a central role in providing information to voters. Campaigns are a communication media where information is transmitted over a number of channels (Berelson, Lazarsfeld, and McPhee, 1954). The information that is provided during campaigns helps to reduce misperceptions and helps voters connect issues with parties, governments, and candidates (Popkin, 1991, p. 41). The central questions are: how do people think during elections? What action can be taken to improve citizens voting decisions?

In the framework of our civic literacy model from Chapter 1, voter education examines the movement from **opinions** to **knowledge**. Combining opinions with knowledge about the parties, candidates, and issues in an election campaign allows voters to take reasonable action and vote for the candidate or party that best represents their views. For example, a voter in Texas in 1994 needed **opinions** and a **knowledge** of issues, candidates, and parties in order to decide whether to vote for Ann Richards or George W. Bush, Jr. for governor. Voters need both opinions and a framework to structure the information they receive during a campaign.

Voters structure their opinions and gather information by talking and listening to others. **Deliberation** is the activity that allows voters and candidates or political organizations to communicate the information used by voters to structure opinions and take appropriate action. During an election campaign, voters are listening to candidates and talking and listening to friends in order to gather the information needed to **participate**.

VOTER OPINION

In campaigns there are two kinds of issues: position and valence. Position issues are those on which a candidate articulates a view for or against a specific policy. In the 1992 presidential campaign, abortion was a position issue with George Bush taking the pro-life position and Bill Clinton the pro-choice view. The term *valence issue* is used for issues on which there is universal agreement or where there is only one side in the debate (Nelson, 1984; Baumgartner and Jones, 1993, Ch 8). The power of valence issues in the 1992 presidential election is illustrated by the *USA TODAY* headline, "At Race's End, Theme Is Trust versus

Change." (November 2, 1992, p. 1) Valence issues require voters to connect a goal or symbol with a particular candidate (Stokes and DiLulio, 1993). They also require solutions. Valence issues provide a clear goal statement, but offer many possible solutions or means to achieve the goal. Although drug control is a valence issue with little debate about the goal, there is debate on whether to control substance abuse by reducing the supply through rigorous law enforcement or by limiting demand through educational programs. In raising a valence issue, candidates must convince voters that their solutions are likely to succeed.

In the 1992 election, the country's economic performance was a valence issue, since nearly everyone wanted a stronger economy. The debate among the candidates was over who could more effectively manage the economic recovery. Stokes and DiLulio conclude, ". . . the dialogue between leaders and led can be democratically legitimate and satisfying, even if it is not centered squarely on position issues and politics." (Stokes and DiLulio, 1993, p. 16) Both valence and position issues are important.

Do voters make their decisions based on past performance or future expectations? Morris Fiorina, in *Retrospective Voting,* argues that voters follow the actions of leaders and parties. If the constituents are satisfied, incumbents are kept in office; otherwise, they are voted out. A more complex analysis requires voters to monitor current performance and calculate what is likely to happen in the future. This is prospective voting. Prospective voting requires predictions.

Voters are capable of prospective decisions on some issues. In making decisions based on economic issues, Michael MacKuen and his colleagues show that voters are more likely to take action based on future expectations than on current or past economic conditions. Their finding indicates a sophisticated level of analysis of the basic data provided by personal experience and government reports. Voters are not fools, and they are fully capable of calculating future advantages based on past performances and personal experience. On economic issues, personal experience may not be as important as one's view of the economy generally (MacKuen, Erikson, and Stimson, 1992).

Whether voters are moved by valence issues or position issues, and whether their judgments are retrospective or prospective, are important issues for both democratic theory and political action. Are voters sophisticated enough to be effective decision makers? Can voters be easily duped by slick candidates? However these questions are resolved, one fact emerges: *clear information helps voters decide whom to support.*

To take action and participate in the voting process, voters need two kinds of information: logistical and political. Logistical information concerns how, when, and where to cast a vote. People need to know the location of their polling place, where to go if they are turned away from the polls, when the polls are open, how to get an absentee ballot, when is the registration deadline, how to use a punch card or voting machine, and who is on the ballot. Without logistical information, even the most politically informed and motivated voter cannot participate.

Second, voters need political information. Political information links candidates, issues, and parties to a voting decision. In 1960, *The American Voter* examined the relationship between candidates, parties, and issues to explain voting behavior (Campbell, Converse, Miller, and Stokes, 1960). *The American Voter* stresses the role of party identification as a psychological organizing principle used to analyze issues and candidates preparatory to the act of voting. Party can be used by the voter to organize other group affiliations, as well as issues and candidates (Campbell, Converse, Miller, and Stokes, 1960, Chapter 12). Fiorina argues that party identification is simply a collection of retrospective judgments about how political parties have performed while in office (Fiorina, 1981).

VOTER ACTION

In politics, talk is action. Students of politics mistakenly report that voting is the most widespread political activity; in fact, talking about politics is a much more common form of political action. Observations about how people talk about politics provide a useful guide to understanding how they think about politics.

William Gamson analyzes how people talk about politics in small group settings. He uses a collective action framework to understand how people talk about politics. The collective action frame proposed by Gamson has three elements:

Injustice. "An injustice frame requires a consciousness of motivated human actors who carry some of the onus for bringing about harm and suffering." There is high emotional content in "moral indignation."

Agency. This "refers to the consciousness that it is possible to alter conditions or policies through collective action.."¡ This framework suggests, "we can do something"; it can also be categorized as "collective efficacy."

Identity. The "process of defining this 'we' typically in opposition to some 'they' who have different interests or values." This is the, "adversarial component" (Gamson, 1992, p. 7.)

Since voter education campaigns seek to provide information that will fit into the voter's cognitive framework, the educational process must be based on political conversations in which groups of people discuss, argue, and share views on political issues of importance to them. In the end, the voter should understand how issues affect his or her life, and whether or not those views are shared by various candidates for public office.

Combining concepts from *The American Voter* and *Talking Politics* produces a better understanding of the role played by candidates, issues, and parties in elections. Table 5.1 shows how candidates, parties, and issues fit into a collective action framework.

TABLE 5.1 Information Needed by Voters

Voter Framework	Party	Candidate	Issue
Political Talk			
Injustice			***
Agency		***	
Identity	***		

Party involves the identification process: "we" are Democrats and "they" are Republicans. The "we" can be racial, ethnic, geographic, or ideological groups. The sociological basis of partisanship is clear. There are clear demographic differences between Republicans and Democrats (Bibby, 1987, p. 267).

Democrats tend to be:	Republicans tend to be:
lower income	higher income
black/Hispanic	white/Asian
catholic/Jewish	protestant
noncollege grads	college graduates
union members	nonunion members
urban	rural/suburban

The Clinton vote mirrors these traditional party differences. Table 5.2 presents results of the national poll of voters as they left the voting booth after participating in the presidential election. Bill Clinton received 55 percent of the Urban vote, 44 percent of the suburban vote, 40 percent of the white vote, 84 percent of the black vote, and 61 percent of the Hispanic vote. The exit poll shows Democrats

TABLE 5.2 Party, Candidate and Voter Preferences in the 1992 Presidential Election

| | VOTED FOR | | | |
	Bush	Clinton	Perot	Total
Party				
Democrat	10%	78%	13%	100
Republican	72%	11%	18%	100
Independent	31%	39%	29%	100
Income level				
Under $15,000	21	61	17	100
$15,000-$29,999	33	47	20	100
$30,000-$49,999	38	42	28	100
$50,000-$74,999	41	41	18	100
Over $75,000	46	37	17	100
Race				
Black	10	84	7	100
Hispanic	26	61	14	100
White	38	40	21	100
Residence				
Urban	32	52	16	100
Suburban	36	44	20	100
Rural	38	43	19	100
Past Votes				
1988 Bush	57%	23%	20%	100
1988 Dukakis	5	84	11	100
1984 Reagan				
Democrats	23	56	21	100
Candidate will bring				
about needed change	20%	50%	47%	

Source: USA Today 11/4/92. Voter Research Surveys exit poll of 15,214 voters on election day.

coming back to the Democratic candidate in 1992 after supporting President Reagan's reelection effort in 1984 (*USA Today*, November 4, 1992).

The close connection between party, issues, and candidates makes identifying the separate impact of these variables on voting decisions very difficult. The 1992 election illustrates this problem.

The voter's reliance on party serves the identity function in Gamson's collective action frame. The "we" and "they" in this case becomes Republicans and Democrats. In some cases, the identification may be with one of the groups mentioned above as closely related to one party or the other. This one element is necessary but not sufficient for action. According to Gamson's schema, agency and injustice must also be present if political thoughts are going to lead to action. *Injustice* is most closely linked to action.

Issues have the capacity to mobilize citizens to action (vote). An issue, when linked both to injustice and to a candidate, provides the motivation for action. The motivational content of issues has not been sufficiently recognized by political scientists. Carmines and Stimson (1980), for example, distinguish between hard and easy issues. Hard issues require a rational weighing of policy alternatives, while easy issues simply identify an end to be achieved. Hard issues require more information and cognitive skill to resolve. Hard or easy issues have the potential to raise the specter of injustice. Position and valence issues, which were described earlier, also may function on an emotional level. The link to injustice is less dependent on content or issue type and more dependent on: how the issue is raised, triggering events, or the social, economic, and political context of the moment. Valence or position issues that contain an element of injustice will be most powerful with the voters.

Candidates are the agents for policy problems and solutions. A successful candidate is able to convince voters that something can be done about a problem if the candidate is elected. Candidate views on valence and position issues are important. Personal characteristics and perceived effectiveness are also salient. Wiessberg and Rusk (1970) show that candidate evaluations are closely connected to issue and party positions. Their study shows that, for challengers, the role of party is weaker, and the role of issues is stronger, than for incumbents. Kinder and Ableson (1981) show that voters evaluate candidates on the basis of competence and integrity. When competence and integrity are added to the voter's positive or negative affect toward the candidate, it is closely related to vote choice. Table 5.2 shows that, in 1992, candidate Bush failed to convince voters that he could bring about needed change. Only 20 percent of the Bush voters thought he would bring needed change, while half of the Clinton voters and 47 percent of the Perot voters saw their candidate as the agent of needed change.

The connection between issues and candidates is demonstrated by looking at the relationship between changes in voters' financial situations and support for a presidential candidate. Quirk and Dalager indicate that those who felt they were better off economically than four years previous voted for George Bush, while those who thought they were worse off cast their vote for Bill Clinton (Quirk and

Dalager, 1993, p. 78). Those in the middle, who felt their family economic situation was about the same, tended to divide their votes evenly between Bush and Clinton. The exit poll from 1992 in Table 5.2 shows that the only income category that favored Bush over Clinton was the relatively small group of people earning more than $75,000 per year.

Voter education is an example of active learning where thinking and action are closely connected. How citizens think about their voting decisions (parties, issues, and candidates) and how they talk about voting (injustice, identity, and agency) must be brought together in an educational process. Citizen knowledge should be structured so voters understand party identity, candidate agency, and issues of injustice. By filling in the cells of Table 5.1, each voter is able to effectively further his or her views at the ballot box.

You, as a voter educator, have created a political resource by creating an informed constituency for your agenda items.

VOTER EDUCATION ACTIVITIES

ACTIVITY 5.1: Informational Pamphlets and Tapes

Prepare flyers, brochures, and videos that explain ballot proposals, summarize candidate positions, or explain how and where to vote. Present issues in a way that shows citizens the impact of their action. For example, a flyer explaining a ballot proposal might say a yes vote means _____ and a no vote means _____. Basic information is vital if voters are expected to determine which policies are fair and which politicians are the voter's best policy agents.

STEP 1: Plan a project to prepare videos and flyers on ballot proposals for the next general election. Don't forget to design a distribution plan for any educational materials you develop. The preparation of videos deserves special comment. They can be produced fairly cheaply (especially in universities that already have the necessary equipment) and can easily be broadcast on cable using local access or local news channels.

STEP 2: Produce the materials outlined in the previous step and contact someone interested in distributing the information. The voter mobilization project described in the next chapter could distribute a wide variety of brochures developed by this activity.

STEP 3: Report to your classmates on the use of materials by other organizations or class members.

STEP 4: Evaluate the educational materials using surveys and focus groups.

ACTIVITY 5.2: Candidate Job Interviews

A central activity in building civic literacy is providing information about candidates and elections because election campaigns play a central role in providing information to voters. Campaigns are a communication medium where information is transmitted over a number of channels. The information that campaigns provide reduces misperceptions and helps voters connect issues with parties, governments, and candidates.

The candidate job interview is an alternative to the debate and to the speech format. The candidates are interviewed separately by three or four citizens representing the prospective employer. If answers are unclear or not satisfactory, follow-up questions are asked immediately. Since most viewers have been interviewed for jobs, they will have the experience to judge the performance of the candidate.

Television is a good medium for the candidate job interview. The interview can be a one-or two-camera live production with a panel of students and a moderator. Rebroadcast on cable systems or PBS stations is possible. You could organize small groups to watch the tape and provide reactions.

STEP 1: Since the use of telecommunication costs money, you must determine what kinds of media production, programing, and publicity resources are available. Apply for support from your college or university, as well as local origination funds from your local cable company or local cable commission. Get a list of candidates from your local election officials. Select which offices you will focus on for this activity.

Step 2: Work with a small group to solicit candidate appearances and to explain the format to the candidates. Establish a publicity committee with linkages to your school PR department, media, and to coalition partners.

STEP 3: Schedule the job interviews and select questioners for each session. You should send each candidate the Urban Agenda Resolution developed in Activity 3. Conduct the interviews.

STEP 4: Work with a study committee to evaluate how this activity succeeded and compare the job interview format with alternative civic literacy activities by the media and political organizations.

The skills developed by these projects are: how to invite candidates to appear at events; how to use a candidate appearance to educate voters; how to ask questions so that specific and relevant answers are given; how to organize the interview; how to mobilize an audience and have the event carried on cable TV and radio; and how to attract media attention for the event.

CHAPTER 6

Voter Mobilization

Political power is built by getting other citizens involved in the political process. Political mobilization is the outcome of a process that successfully recruits people into politics (Tilly, 1978). Political organizations recruit people for a wide variety of actions. Recruitment may be aimed at motivating people to vote, requesting that they contact their elected officials, or that they protest a governmental action. These activities are aimed at specific political goals. Political activists believe that a mobilizing organization is "a vehicle of power." Political mobilization and subsequent political activity can create political resources that are used to alter the distribution of power.

IMPACT OF MOBILIZATION

The goal of mobilization is to recruit others to political **participation**. Chapter 5 discussed how opinions are structured during educational campaigns; this chapter emphasizes how action is structured through mobilization of citizens to participate in the political process. **Participation**, the fourth element of civic literacy, combines structure and action. The amount of structure in any political action can vary considerably. For example, in voter registration, action might be a loosely organized effort to ask friends or co-workers to register. In mobilization, organized structures play a more prominent role. People are targeted for mobilization, and efforts are planned strategically (the **knowledge** element of civic literacy). Once a group or area is targeted for mobilization, a corps of volunteers are recruited, organized with assignments, and sent in to conduct the campaign.

This chapter explores the structures and processes that facilitate participation in politics and presents activities designed to enhance mobilization skills. We begin with a discussion of what is known about participation and the role of groups in encouraging citizens to vote.

People are likely to participate in elections when they are asked. Rosenstone and Hansen report that in presidential elections from 1956–1988, 74.6 percent of the people reporting they were contacted by a political party voted, while only 66.8 percent who reported no contact voted. In the midterm congressional elections 57.3 percent of party-contacted voters voted, while only 46.9 percent of the noncontacted voters voted (Rosenstone and Hansen, 1993, p. 171.).

Mobilization makes a difference in turnout. Even with the demographic factors and political attitudes taken into account, there is an impact for mobilization in increasing turnout. Research on congressional elections points to two variables from the political environment that significantly affect the probability of mobilization. First, voter registration laws, which we reviewed in Chapter 4, are significantly related to turnout. Second, the election campaign itself is important. An open congressional seat and an election with more money spent will have higher turnout (Jackson, 1993, p. 1088). Competitive elections and increases in the amount of money spent increase mobilization. Election campaigns and political parties reduce the barriers to participation by making information more accessible, by reminding people to vote, and by providing logistical information and assistance (Jackson, 1993).

MOBILIZATION GROUPS

The role of political parties in asking people to participate in politics is critical. The principal function of the party organizations is to contest elections by mobilizing voters (Eldersveld, 1964). In his study of Detroit political parties, Eldersveld shows a direct connection between exposure to political parties and the potential for activism. Conversely, when party exposure declines, so does the potential for activism.

The ability of parties to mobilize voters depends on the local organization and its organizers. Eldersveld presents data on gaps in what the local workers actually do. Registration, house-to-house canvassing, and election-day round-up are the three critical tasks for precinct workers. Only 17 percent of the Democrats and 25 percent of the Republicans reported doing all three tasks in Detroit during the 1950s (Eldersveld, 1964, pp. 350-51).

Making matters worse is the decline in the number of precinct positions filled. In 1988, we found that 60 percent of the precinct delegates for the political parties in the Detroit area were vacant. Eldersveld's 1957 survey of Republican and Democratic precinct captains or delegates in the same area had a response rate of 85.6 percent. (Eldersveld, 1964, p. 26) This sharp decline in capacity of parties to activate citizens locally is disturbing.

Since 1970, two important trends have occurred:

1. There has been a sharp decline in the numbers of voters contacted by the major political parties. Party contact peaked in 1982 when the Republicans and Democrats together contacted slightly less than 35 percent of the electorate. By 1990 the major parties contacted less than 20 percent of the voters.

2. The effectiveness of party contact has improved dramatically. To measure party effectiveness, it is necessary simply to subtract the percentage of people contacted who voted from the percent of people not contacted who voted (Weilhouwer and Lockerbie, 1994, p. 214). Using the figures from 1952–1988 quoted above, average effectiveness for presidential elections is 7.8 (74.6 percent–66.8 percent) and the average effectiveness for midterm elections is 10.4 (57.3 percent 46.9 percent). Using this measure, party effectiveness has nearly doubled from 17 in 1984 to 31 in 1990. Improved effectiveness and decreasing contacts mean political parties are concentrating efforts on those who are likely to participate and are reaching them with messages linked to behavior.

We can only speculate on whether, if more people were contacted, parties would be equally effective. Eldersveld's findings discussed above lead to the expectation that if more were contacted, more would participate, even if efficiency declined.

Political parties are not the only political groups trying to mobilize voters. Interest groups use "indirect lobbying" campaigns to mobilize members to apply political pressure on elected officials during election campaigns (Walker, 1991, Chapter 6). Indirect lobbying by interest groups takes many forms, including: campaign contributions through Political Action Groups, letter writing campaigns by members to key officials, contacting members with suggestions on how to vote, and having members participate in election campaigns on behalf of preferred candidates.

Interest groups have a mobilization advantage because they can represent a narrow issue area and attract citizens who share their view. Interest groups often survey members to determine opinions before engaging in a lobbying campaign. Lobbying is used by interest groups as a mobilization tactic. For example, BoatUS, an organization representing boat owners, used their opposition to increased recreational boat taxes and user fees to recruit new members.

Neighborhood and community groups have also used political mobilization techniques to draw attention to local issues. These organizations have been successful in combining election mobilization with informal contacts with office holders (Barry, Portney, and Thomson, 1993). The grass-roots characteristic of these groups gives them a powerful potential for mobilizing citizens to political action.

Piven and Cloward observe that elections are the first stage of protest (1977, p. 15). Protest movements for civil rights (Piven and Cloward, 1977; and Rosenstone and Hansen, 1993); welfare reform (Piven and Cloward, 1977); environmental protection and nuclear power (Jones and Baumgartner, 1993); and farm workers (Jenkins, 1985) have employed election strategies as a tactic to gain political power. Mobilizing supporters and increasing the visibility of issues are the primary goals of protest group participation in the electoral process.

Candidate organizations are increasingly important in voter mobilization efforts (Bibby 1987, p. 230). Unlike more formal party organizations, which depend on local volunteers to canvass voters and distribute flyers, candidate organizations rely on professionals for polling and utilize media consultants or direct mail experts for voter contact. Although candidate organizations may mobilize voters, their paid staff and temporary nature actually reduce the possibility for voluntary political action. Resources, such as money and people, that could go into a permanent voluntary organization are thus sapped away into a shadow organization.

MOBILIZATION PLAN

In order to create an effective framework for mobilizing voters, three questions must be answered:

1. What is the mobilization strategy?
2. Who should we mobilize?
3. Which methods of mobilization are effective?

1. What is the mobilization strategy?

The basic strategic question is how widely to spread your mobilization efforts. Should you try to convert and mobilize potentially hostile voters or should you simply mobilize your sure supporters? The answers to these questions depend on the political environment and the strength of the organization in that environment. If you are running the campaign of a minority party candidate, your best strategy is to broaden the appeal; however, if you are running the campaign of a majority party candidate you can afford simply to mobilize your supporters (Goldenberg and Traugott, 1984, p. 48).

Congressional campaign managers report that mobilization strategies are a function of the competitiveness of the election (open seats or races against incumbents); the probability of success (sure winners, hopefuls, those who are vulnerable, and sure losers); and party. Party differences are important. No matter what kind of race they are in, Republicans are more likely to try to convert voters than Democrats. Among Democrats, as uncertainty increases, so do appeals to broader constituencies. Challengers have broader appeal than incumbents (Goldenberg and Traugott, 1984, p. 49).

2. Who should we mobilize?

Rosenstone and Hansen identify the kinds of voters that political parties are most likely to mobilize.

1. Voters who are most likely to support the party's candidates.
2. Voters who are centrally located in social networks (for example, those who have lived in a community for a long time or who belong to community groups).
3. Voters who have demographic and attitudinal factors associated with voting (highly educated, high income, white).
4. Voter's history in previous elections. Voters who have consistently participated in previous elections are most likely to participate in this one. One simple, and common, method is to map voter turnout (percent of eligible voters voting) by precinct and to expend resources only on mobilizing high turnout areas (Rosenstone and Hansen, 1993, pp. 163-166).

Studies of political participation provide a clear description of the easiest mobilization target based on personal characteristics.

Social and economic factors are closely related to the likelihood of voting. Education, age, income, occupation, and race all play an important role in determining who votes and who doesn't vote (Wolfinger and Rosenstone, 1980, Chapters 13; Asher, 1988, p. 55; and Teixeira, 1993, Chapter 3). Well-educated, older, employed, white people are more likely to be voters than people without these characteristics.

Education seems to be the most useful variable for targeting likely voters (Milbrath, 1965 and Jackson, 1993). Voters with more education are likely to understand their stake in politics, are more likely to be exposed to information, and are more capable of using the political information they have (Wolfinger and Rosenstone, 1980, p. 180).

The strength of partisan identification is also an extremely useful bit of information for finding easily mobilizable voters. As partisanship intensifies, the probability of voting increases (Campbell, Converse, Miller, and Stokes, 1960; Asher, 1988; Jackson, 1993; Wolfinger and Rosenstone, 1980). Issues can also be powerful instruments of mobilization, as in the case of the California tax revolt of 1978 (Rosenstone and Hansen, 1993, p. 106). Unfortunately, attitudinal variables require surveys, which are very expensive.

3. Which methods of mobilization are effective?

Mobilization methods are either direct or indirect. Direct mobilization recruits people for participation through a contact with the participation target (voter or activist). Indirect mobilization uses social networks to mobilize people to political action.

Evidence of indirect mobilization's impact is provided by the congressional campaign managers studied by Goldenberg and Traugott. Seventy-two percent of the campaign managers identified local groups that were important to the outcome of the election. They report that the following groups were important: unions (mentioned by 48 percent), black and Hispanic groups (mentioned by 18 percent), business groups (mentioned by 17 percent), and women's groups (mentioned by 15 percent) (Goldenberg and Traugott, 1984, p. 31). The networks indirectly mobilized show considerable variation. Even former political science graduate students have been mobilized to help congressional candidates.

There are three types of direct contact political organizations have with voters: mass media, direct mail, and personal contact. These three methods differ in the degree to which the message is personalized for the voter. Personal contact is designed to determine and answer individual voter concerns. Mass media campaigns present a message and hope (or, based on research, predict) to hit a sympathetic cord with the voter. In their survey of congressional campaign managers, Goldenberg and Traugott found personal contact used in 95 percent of campaigns, direct mail used in 70 percent, newspaper ads used in 78 percent, radio ads used in 65 percent, and TV ads used in 44 percent (Goldenberg and Traugott, 1984, p. 116).

Studies from 1927 to the present show that the type of contact is closely related to success. Personal contact (as opposed to mailings, phones, or media) has the greatest chance of success (Gosnell, 1927; Eldersveld, 1956, pp. 154–165; Huckfeldt and Sprague, 1992, pp.70–86).

The best resource for discussion of this topic is candidates for office in your area. Ask candidates for elected office how they campaign and whether they believe direct contact is more important than mailings or media. Also ask politically active organizations to explain how they mobilize voters and recruit participants. Design strategies for various groups in your community. What about your state legislators and congresspersons?

VOTER MOBILIZATION ACTIVITIES

Two projects are outlined to stimulate your understanding of political mobilization. One is the Voter Mobilization Project and the second is the Student Campaign Involvement Project. These projects are designed to teach you the skills necessary to build an organization whose goal is to increase political participation.

ACTIVITY 6.1: Voter Mobilization Project

Your activity is the Voter Education Project. This project establishes Voter Education and Participation Centers in host organizations such as churches, senior citizen centers, neighborhood centers, union halls, shopping centers, and stores. Each center is staffed by students working with volunteers from the host organization. Host organizations are nonpartisan. Each center initiates voter contact to alert citizens to an upcoming election, explains voting procedures, offers help with absentee voter applications, and mobilizes citizens to vote on election day through canvassing and transportation or day care assistance.

STEP 1: Recruit participating organizations. During the 1992 elections the Voter Education Project in Michigan recruited eight organizations in the Detroit area to establish Voter Education and

Participation Centers. Each host organization commits volunteers to work at specific times to disseminate information and canvass with students in targeted areas. You will also cooperate with host organizations to keep track of the time you work.

STEP 2: Target key precincts to work in. The ideal method for targeting precincts is to combine census data with precinct participation reports. These data allow you to target precincts based on both those demographic characteristics that predict turnout and also historical patterns of voting in an area. Since the Voter Education Project in Michigan did not have census and precinct data, we targeted precincts based only on historical voting data. We gave high priority to precincts that had at least 1,500 registered voters and that had produced at least 250 votes in the most recent mayoral election. In the city of Detroit, this selection method targeted 61 out of 450 precincts.

STEP 3: Each student must find a specific organization to work in. Try to find centers with clearly defined hours of operation so that you can fit this activity into your schedules.

STEP 4: Map preelection day and election day strategy with other students and organizations. With so many activities (canvassing, absent voter applications, information dissemination, and explaining voting procedures), it is important that you and your host organization establish activity priorities and schedules. If the host organization is a senior citizen center, they may emphasize absent voter applications. A church, on the other hand, may place a high priority on canvassing people in the neighborhood.

STEP 5: Implement strategies. Preelection and election day activities must be planned and scheduled well in advance. The goals for these activities are to target and inform voters before the election and to get them to the polls on election day. Each Voter Education and Participation Center will have student and volunteer cochairs who will be responsible for organizing and mobilizing the workers.

Preelection day activities consist of making lists of voters you want to contact on election day. You can start with membership lists, voter registration lists, or no list at all, but by election day you should have a list of citizens you want to see vote. The three weeks prior to an election is a period of intensive voter contact and information gathering. The type of contact depends on the resources available (personnel, phones, offices, and computers). This is a good time to publicize the Voter Education and Participation Center number, which voters who need assistance on election day can call.

Election day activities are focused on getting out the vote. The early morning is spent putting the organization in place. This may mean assigning workers to polling places to check off voters when they vote or having people in the center available to assist voters in getting to the polls. The afternoon is devoted to determining which voters need to be reminded to vote. The most critical time on election day is from 4 P.M. until the polls close. During this time, efforts need to be made to contact any voter who has not voted and remind him or her to vote—the election will be over soon and it will be too late to vote.

STEP 6: An activity as complex as voter mobilization requires a variety of reports to be sure it is running successfully. You should report on the number of hours you worked, the number of voters you contacted, and the percent of the assigned area in which the canvass is complete. The project should collect election day responses as well as election turnout statistics by precinct.

STEP 7: You will help conduct an analysis at your Voter Education and Participation Center based on the reports outlined in Step 6. Strategies for the next mobilization effort should be planned at this time. You will also participate in a project-level meeting held to evaluate the performance of each center and the project as a whole. This is the one time when all of the Voter Education and Participation Center groups may want to come together to share their experiences.

ACTIVITY 6.2: Student Campaign Involvement Project

The second action option is to create opportunities for voter participation in campaigns, parties, or issue movements. This activity can be implemented through the four-step process:

STEP 1: Candidate organizations, political parties, interest groups, and issue movements are recruited to use students in their election efforts. During general elections, political party headquarters have lists of campaign managers who serve as contact points to recruit student volunteers. Other groups are listed in the phone book or are known to locally active political workers. Students themselves are an excellent source of information on politically active organizations. Most groups are willing to have volunteers but need to be made aware of the educational goals of the participation.

STEP 2: Class members are provided with information and campaign contacts to facilitate participation in electoral activity. At this stage, it is often useful to set up a candidate forum where candidates and campaign managers can recruit student workers. Meetings are set up for students and campaigns to begin working together.

STEP 3: Student experience is monitored through class discussion. The experience of the groups using students is monitored through phone conversations and meetings. Students are responsible for writing a report of their experience. Reports must describe the student's experience and evaluate the overall strategy of the campaign.

STEP 4: After the election, the experience of groups and students is evaluated through surveys and class discussions which include campaign managers and students.

Partisan and nonpartisan mobilization efforts require high levels of organization and mobilization among the action skills and advocacy and analysis among the information skills. Efficient and accountable organizations are required to turn out voters on election day. Analysis of voting patterns as a guide to strategy and evaluation of election results and organizational effectiveness are essential components of this activity.

CHAPTER 7

Public Accountability

Democracy means public power. Citizen control of governmental institutions and decisions is the fundamental tenet of democratic theory. How can you build power so the political system will hear and act on your demands?

Our model of civic literacy provides a tool for analyzing this question. Each of the four components of civic literacy (opinions, deliberation, knowledge, and activity) are needed to construct a responsive government. The steps toward responsive policy making are:

STEP 1 Opinion. Citizen opinions are measured.

STEP 2 Deliberation. Opinions are expressed; elites and policy makers listen to these opinions and share their own concerns.

STEP 3 Knowledge. Policymaker's decisions are monitored and evaluated by citizen groups, based on discussions in step 2.

STEP 4 Participation. Policy decisions are made.

Democracy requires a connection between steps 1 and 4 (opinions and policy actions). Central to building this connection is a deliberative process in which leaders and citizens exchange opinions and acquire knowledge about problems and solutions. The New England town meeting represents a structured approach to this process. In the town meeting, citizens come together to decide on issues such as the town budget and new town ordinances, as well as to elect town officials. What comes out of these meetings is a close communication between citizens and their elected leaders. While these steps describe a normative theory of responsive government, the reality is more complicated.

Do citizens control their government? Although the question is simple, the answers are complex. Understanding the power of citizens over their government requires examination of several issues: are public opinions coherent enough to act on? Are policies stable enough to be measured and understood by the public? Is there a connection between public opinion and public policy? What is the connection? What kinds of government decisions and institutions are open to public influence? How can policies be changed? How can public actions be evaluated by citizens? These questions are not easy to answer, but they are critical to understanding how to live and act in a democracy.

CITIZEN OPINION

The concept of democratic representation links the public's thinking with governmental action. The public's thinking is measured by collecting individual opinions. Governmental action is making policy choices and decisions.

How these variables are aggregated and described are important issues that influence conclusions about democratic government. Miller and Stokes, for example, link constituency opinion (measured by surveys and aggregated by average scores) with congressional roll-call votes (measured by key recorded votes on a variety of issues) as a way of understanding representative democracy (Miller and Stokes, 1964). Erikson, Wright, and McIver (1993) use state public opinion measurements and state policy in several areas to show the impact of opinion on policy. McDonagh (1992) studies the role of district opinion (measured by state referendum votes) on roll-call voting (using important labor and suffrage votes) from 1913–1917.

Are public opinions coherent enough to act on?

The answer to this question is yes and no, depending on what criteria and measurements are employed.

The **no** part of the answer is based on the fact that public knowledge about policy and politics is very low; individual attitudes are unstable and unreliable; and there is little connection between issue positions and voting behavior on the part of many citizens. Early studies of voting behavior show that people do not pay much attention to campaigns, are confused about where candidates stand on critical issues (Berelson, Lazarsfeld, and McPhee, 1954), do not know where the political parties stand, or what the government is currently doing or even what they want the government to do on critical issues (Campbell, Converse, Miller, and Stokes, 1960). In 1956, voters were given a list of sixteen issues and asked if they had an opinion and if they knew what the government was currently doing in each area. The list contained issues from foreign policy to insuring medical care. Only about 60 percent of those surveyed both had an opinion and reported knowing what the government was doing on an issue. The accuracy of this knowledge was not measured (Campbell, Converse, Miller, and Stokes, 1960, p. 174).

The instability of voters' attitudes over time is documented by two panel studies, which interviewed the same people at three points in time (1956, 1958, 1960, and 1972, 1974, 1976) (Converse, 1964; and Converse and Markus, 1979). As an example of attitude instability, they examined opinions on school desegregation. In 1954, the Supreme Court declared racially segregated schools unconstitutional and directed the federal government to desegregate the schools with all deliberate speed. *The American Voter* reports that, in 1956, 12 percent had no opinion on school segregation, 34 percent had an opinion but did not know what the government was doing, and 54 percent both had an opinion and knew what the government was doing (Campbell, Converse, Miller, and Stokes, 1960, p. 174). In the panel study (1956, 58, 60), only 37 percent gave consistent agree or disagree answers for all three interviews on the question of whether the government should stay out of the school segregation issue. On this question, 38 percent did not express an opinion in at least one interview and 25 percent gave inconsistent responses (Page and Shapiro, 1992, p. 7).

The **yes** part of the answer is that although individual opinions are unstable and uninformed, collective opinions are stable and react in a rational way to external events and conditions. Page and Shapiro argue in a section entitled, "From Individual Ignorance to Collective Wisdom", ". . . the measurement of collective public opinion is largely free of the random error associated with individual opinions." (p. 16) Later, these authors conclude, "Even though individuals may often hold only weak and poorly informed opinions, subject to measurement error and random changes due to new information, there can still exist a stable, meaningful public opinion based on the underlying central tendencies of individuals' opinions" (Page and Shapiro, 1992, p. 26).

Another method of collecting opinions is to aggregate across issues (instead of individuals). Here we look for broader themes on which the public might have more stable and enduring preferences. The term *attitude structure* is defined as, ". . . two or more beliefs or opinions held by an individual [which] are in some way or another functionally related" (Campbell, Converse, Miller, and Stokes, 1960, p. 198). Initial efforts by Converse and his colleagues to combine opinions on various policy issues into ideologies showed little consistency across issues. There is not much evidence that opinions on narrow policy issues cluster together to form an ideology along the lines of a liberal-conservative continuum (Converse, 1964).

Stimson uses the term "policy mood" to capture a less confining form for structuring opinions about specific policies (1991). The prevailing policy mood, he argues, is our view toward government. Policy preferences on health care, urban problems, welfare, education, and racial equality move in parallel as public support for government action has surged and declined. These issue tracks are so powerful that movement in one leads to movement in others. After the urban riots in the late 1960s, support for government action in areas such as health care and education declined. By 1990, support of government action in health care pushed up the support for government action in areas such as urban problems.

MEASURING WHAT GOVERNMENT DECIDES (POLICY)

This brings us to the issue of measuring governmental decisions. The most commonly used policy measure is legislative roll-call votes. Roll-call votes have the advantage of being public, recorded, and related to substantive issues. They have the disadvantage of being only the formal ratification of decisions reached elsewhere. Nevertheless, roll-call votes have been used to examine a wide variety of opinion and policy connections including: support for progressive era legislation in areas of labor reform, antitrust regulation, suffrage, and prohibition (McDonagh, 1992); 1950s-era issues including foreign policy, civil rights, and social welfare (Miller and Stokes, 1964); and liberal and conservative ideologies from 1964–1990 (Stimson, MacKuen, and Erickson, 1994). The use of roll-call votes is not limited to the legislative arena. Since the president takes positions on roll-call votes, his score on policy dimensions can be calculated and related to public opinion.

Another frequently used policy measure is money. Expenditures in various policy categories such as welfare or economic development have been analyzed across states, within states, and within local governments (Dye, 1966; Anton, 1989; Chesney, 1994).

State-level policies have been quantitatively measured and analyzed. Erickson, Wright, and McIver (1993) produced an Index Composite Policy Liberalism for states based on eight variables: 1. per-pupil spending for education, 2. scope of Medicaid benefits, 3. scope eligibility for Aid to Families with Dependent Children (AFDC), 4. responsiveness to consumer protection, 5. use of liberal approaches to criminal justice, 6. legalized gambling, 7. speed of Equal Rights Amendment ratification, and 8. tax progressivism (Erickson, Wright, and McIver, 1993 pp. 75–77). Since these variables were highly related, a single score combining these policies could be produced.

In their examination of democracy in five urban areas, Berry, Portney, and Thomson (1993) produced a detailed measure for policy outcomes at the local level. Their goal was to measure how issues were resolved by local governments. Using interviews with knowledgeable people, and studying newspaper reports and meeting reports, they were able to determine how (in what direction) each issue was resolved in each city. For example, in San Antonio, one issue was the proposed sale of the publicly owned gas and electric company to a private concern. The city council did not sell the utility (see Berry, Portney, and Thomson, 1993, Appendix 6.1). Local policy decisions such as homelessness, riverfront development, crime, downtown parking, and football stadium funding are examined using this approach. A significant drawback of this approach is the large amount of time and effort required to determine policy outcomes in several areas and in several localities. This detailed policy description has been used at the national level to analyze policies in specific areas such as health care (Jacobs, 1993; Skocpol, 1994), but an analysis across several issues requires more time and money than has been available.

A more comprehensive approach is suggested in Robert Putnam's study of regional governments in Italy. He measures effectiveness on three dimensions: policy process (cabinet stability, budget promptness, and statistical and information services); policy content (reform legislation on economic development, environmental planning, and social services, and legislative innovation in twelve policy areas); policy implementation (day-care centers, family clinics, industrial policy instruments, agricultural spending capacity, local health-unit expenditures, housing and urban development, and bureaucratic responsiveness) (pp. 67–73). These twelve factors are combined to form an institutional performance index. As a test of the validity of the index, Putnam asked citizens to rank their institutions as well. The correlation between the objective measures and the citizen opinions is a high .84 (Putnam, 1993, p. 77). The stability of the index over time is also quite high.

REPRESENTATION: LINKING OPINIONS AND POLICY

Is there a connection between public opinion and public policy? The answer is yes.

A wide variety of studies have shown a linkage between public opinion and public policy. The most common measurement of this relationship is the correlation between opinion and decisions. For example, Miller and Stokes report a .65 correlation coefficient between constituency opinion and roll-call votes for civil rights issues. Stimson, MacKuen, and Erickson correlate indicators of policy liberalism taken from roll-call votes with the global opinion discussed above. They report correlations of .47 for the Senate and .39 for the House of Representatives.

The connection between state policy and public opinion is very strong according to Erickson, Wright, and McIver (1993). They report the relationship between their Composite Liberalism Index and state liberal public opinion (measured by an adjusted correlation) as a very high .91. In fact, state opinion is more closely related to policy than economic variables used in previous studies to explain why states choose specific policies.

In their study of urban democracy, Berry, Portney, and Thomson examine the connection between public opinion and the policy decisions outlined above. The proportion of people who wanted the issue resolved in the way it was varied from 13 percent wanting increased city spending in Dayton to 91 percent against legalization of crack and cocaine in Portland. City averages varied from a high of 62 percent opinion-policy agreement in Portland to a low of 40 percent in San Antonio (Berry, Portney and Thomson, 1993, p. 154).

The precise nature of the opinion-policy connection, the causal order (which came first, the opinion or the policy?), and the conditions under which it operates most effectively remain issues for debate among scholars and activists. The connection between opinion and policy can be easily overestimated because of variables such as demographics, leadership characteristics, political culture and party influence, as well as organized interest groups and social movements, which strengthen the relationship by being related to both opinion and policy. In the context of civic literacy, a precise correlation or regression estimate of the relationship and the causal order are less important, while the conditions for strengthening the connection between opinion and policy are much more important.

Controversial issues produce a strong link between public opinion and policy behavior. Miller and Stokes' analysis shows a much stronger relationship between roll-call votes and constituency opinion on issues viewed as controversial by members of Congress (such as civil rights). The role of paranoia in producing representative government is high. Even when the probability of defeat is low, the fear of defeat can be quite high and can keep even safe representatives in touch with their constituents. Politicians are conservative (risk adverse) when it comes to election defeat.

Representation runs along a continuum from doing favors for constituents (*errands* is the term used by Eulau and Prewitt) to promoting substantive policy issues and solutions. Members of Congress tend to represent their districts either by servicing constituent demands or by promoting substantive legislation in the interest of the district. These embody two career paths members of Congress can choose (Fenno, 1978).

There has been some dispute over whether these forms of representation are complementary or in conflict. In a study of San Fransico-area city councils, running errands and substantive representation were complementary. Councils that did not provide constituent services were also unlikely to respond to substantive groups that presented demands for action (Eulau and Prewitt, 1973). In contrast, Fenno's study of Congress shows service and substantive styles are in conflict. A representative with a fixed amount of time must choose one or the other style.

Two additional bits of information help to solve this puzzle. First, in his study of Italian regional governments Robert Putnam finds a negative relationship between "particularized contacting" ("running errands" in Eulau and Prewitt) and government effectiveness. Time spent trying to get or give jobs to one's cronies seems to deter government performance. For Putnam, the issue is not time, it is politics (1993). Regions with particularized contacting are characterized by hierarchy patron-client relationships; while areas with stronger associational ties or grass roots organizations have more programmatic contacting.

Second, in their study of agenda setting, Baumgartner and Jones conclude that translating individual-level concerns to the level of a substantive policy concern is a vital step. They state, "Private problems need to be linked to public causes in order to demand governmental attention"(1993, p. 27). A significant obstacle to both political action and to representation is the reluctance of people to translate their personal problems into policy concerns. An individual who wrecks a tire (or an axle) in a pothole has an individual problem, which may become a public problem if other people have the same experiences. Many city elections are won or lost on potholes or snow removal (Mayor Byrne was defeated on this issue in Chicago).

Effective representation and effective government both depend on the translation of individual citizens' problems into publicly relevant issues. Systems that do not facilitate such transmission are, simply, ineffective. Systems that only reach the service level of representation fail to serve a primary function of democracy, which is to aggregate citizen demands into policy. Any political system has a variety of mechanisms that facilitate the transmission of opinion to policy.

POWER AND RESPONSIVENESS

Clearly, political systems aggregate demands unequally. The basic question of politics is: Who gets what? Translated into our discussion, this question becomes: Whose opinions become policy? Some demands are treated with more respect than others. Whether an opinion is translated into policy by the political system is a function of: the opinion, the group which is aggregating the opinion, and other political elites.

The political system is responsive to those with: power (money, votes, or information), positive images, and effective political strategies. Even among emerging political organizations, there are clear power differences. Groups start with friends. Finding a wealthy benefactor (individual or group) is a significant advantage for political success (Walker, 1991).

Whether the target population for a policy is viewed positively or negatively influences what tools are chosen to deal with the problem. Even powerful groups that are viewed negatively are not able to control their policy outcomes. These groups will suffer from overt and symbolic burdens from public policy (Schneider, and Ingram, 1993).

Groups also can succeed or fail due to their political strategy. Walker contends that large groups with subunit membership organizations can afford either an inside strategy or an outside strategy. However, a small group with no subunit memberships will be limited to an inside strategy and would only waste their limited resources by going outside (Walker, 1991).

POLITICAL LEADERSHIP

Standing between the public's opinions and policy decisions are a variety of political leaders whose goal is to acquire political power over the decisions being made. Byron Jones distinguishes between leadership in structured and unstructured situations. This view is consistent with our model of civic literacy, which distinguishes between action in structured and unstructured (citizen) arenas. Jones uses the term *transactional entrepreneur* for the leader in a structured situation and the term *transforming entrepreneur* for the leader outside structured situations. His definitions are:

> The transactional entrepreneur offers up new policies or strategies within the existing set of rules that will subtly modify the system. Transforming entrepreneurs define new political realities for followers. (Jones, 1989, p. 293).

Transformational leadership takes the opinions and deliberation components of civic literacy and builds political power. This task is accomplished in the agenda-setting process, where deliberation turns private citizen opinions into statements of policy problems. In this process, opinions are mobilized in a structure created by the transformational leader.

Transactional leaders understand how to channel knowledge and participation to further their acquision of power. The key resources for leaders to remain in the political structure are voter registration, voter education, and voter mobilization activities. Members of Congress are primarily transactional leaders. Do you remember Richard Fenno's description of the campaign-governing-campaign cycle, which was discussed in Chapter 2? In his model, representatives communicate with voters and make policy decisions within the structure of political institutions. They hope their actions will generate voter support.

What is the relation between transactional and transforming leaders? Clues to this relationship are found in studies of political parties. Parties are interesting because they contain both elected officials (transactional leaders) and party activists (transformational leaders). Summarizing this relationship in state political party organizations, Erikson, Wright, and McIver observe, "In actuality state parties, like national parties, are pushed toward the median voter position by electoral considerations and away from the median voter position by the preferences of their activists" (Erikson, Wright, and McIver, 1993).

Transformational leaders are also supplied by interest groups. In local politics, business leaders often perform the transactional role (Berry, Portney and Thomson, 1993). Business leaders often have the resources (time, money, and networks) necessary for transactional leadership. Competition between transformational leaders can take place as it did in San Antonio between local business leaders, national/international leaders, and the Hispanic community. Transformational leaders representing these new interests brought a new transaction leader, Henry Cisneros, to power (Jones, 1989; Berry, Portney, and Thomson, 1993).

Responsive political systems depend on a close connection between transforming and transaction leaders. The decline of these connections in political parties may require initiating new structures that can bring these leaders together in a sustained deliberative process.

A Case of Leadership Failure: National League of Cities Agenda

In 1988, the National League of Cities(NLC), representing 10,000 mayors and city council members, sought to place the issue of an urban crisis on the public agenda. The league published *Election '88: Investing in Home Town America,* that listed ten issues which made up the urban crisis. The ten issues were: education, drug abuse, poverty, children at risk, jobs and job training, the urban infrastructure, housing and neighborhoods, crime, ensuring survival for all people, and partnership between federal, state, and local governments in dealing with this crisis. Each of these themes was demonstrated by a few dramatic statistics and was followed by two questions: What should the federal government do? What should it do first? The NLC wanted these questions answered by each candidate for president in 1988.

The facts behind these ten issues clearly indicated that urban needs were not being met. The development of a document by the NLC turned these unmet needs into demands. By linking the ten issues, it was hoped that the state of America's towns and cities would get on the political agenda.

The effort to place urban issues on the political agenda in 1988 failed. No candidate responded to the questions put forth by the National League of Cities. Since neither presidential candidate endorsed the urban agenda in 1988, it is not surprising that there was virtually no action taken in this policy area between 1988 and 1992. The interesting political question is: Why did this effort fail? Before speculating on why the Urban Agenda failed, we must analyze the agenda formation process.

The agenda presented by the NLC had some political advantages when it was first presented in 1988. First, it stated broad problems in a way that would protect the agenda from debate over specific solutions. Second, it had the support of a large social group: urban dwellers. Third, it had the active support of locally elected officials with political access to national candidates and the national media.

However, there was a failure of political leadership. The fact that the Urban Agenda in 1988 did not attain national recognition can be traced to the failure to connect transactional and transformation leaders. The transaction leaders were the presidential candidates (Governor Dukakis and Vice President Bush); the transformation leaders were Jesse Jackson and New York Mayor Ed Koch.

Koch's strategy was to urge fellow municipal officials to withhold support from candidates who did not endorse the Urban Agenda. Since most municipal officials are transaction leaders, it is not surprising that they did not use this opportunity to demonstrate their clout or mobilize their voters.

Reverend Jackson, on the other hand, did engage in an effort to mobilize voters around this agenda. He conducted his mobilization effort within the Democratic party. Jackson's success in recruiting new voters did not move the transaction leaders to the Urban Agenda. The Dukakis campaign calculated that the Jackson recruits were unlikely to vote for Bush and therefore did not have to be courted to vote Democratic. Feinstein has argued that Dukakis would have won a majority of the electoral college if he had adopted the Urban Agenda and campaigned aggressively in urban areas (Feinstein, 1992).

Urban transformation leaders did not fare any better in the 1992 campaign than they had in 1988. Neither President Bush nor Governor Clinton nor Ross Perot stressed urban issues or campaigned aggressively in urban areas. Transaction leaders apparently decided that would be counterproductive. The irony for President Clinton's reelection strategy is that in 1992 he won a majority of urban votes, but at the same time the absolute number of votes produced for him in the 130 most urban counties in the country declined, compared to the 1988 Democratic candidate.

Some transaction leaders have decided that simply ignoring urban issues is not an effective strategy. Leaders in the Republican-dominated 104th Congress are making antiurbanism an agenda item. Newspapers carrying headlines such as "GOP Targets Urban Aid" (Detroit Free Press 11/14/94) deliver this message clearly.

Representative democracy is based on the assumption that citizens will monitor and evaluate the performance of the elected officials AND that elected officials care what citizens think. A neat division of responsibility is the transactional leader's interest in voter's views and the transformation leader's interest in evaluating policy decisions.

For citizens effectively to control public institutions and decision makers, they must be able to perform competent evaluations and discuss the results with transactional leaders. Three basic characteristics of evaluation research are that information must be: timely, relevant to the decision at hand, and address items that are within the control of policy makers (Rossi and Freeman, 1982). Evaluation must occur at the proper point in the political cycle, must be based on established criteria, must be based on accurate measurement and data collection, and the results and conclusions must be widely disseminated. Political support for the evaluation's conclusion is also an important factor in gaining acceptance for your conclusions.

ACCOUNTABILITY ACTIVITY

Accountability requires a vehicle whereby transformation leaders can express collective opinions and have candidates (transaction leaders) respond in a way that gives voters an opportunity to evaluate the views presented by both kinds of leader. The leader's deliberation is ideally based on evaluation of current government and programatic performance. Connecting both types of leaders with voters produces representative government. The following activity is one way to organize a forum to improve representation.

ACTIVITY 7.1: Create an Accountability Catalyst

Create an accountability catalyst by recruiting community leaders to develop an agenda and hold candidate forums. This activity uses elements from each of the previous activities. A timetable for this activity is:

STEP 1: During January of election year, work with other students to recruit community leaders to meet and formulate an issue agenda. Leaders can be effectively recruited using grass-roots organizing principles. Start with a group of twelve, and ask each one to recruit an additional six participants.

STEP 2: During February to April of election year, along with other classmates, hold small and intermediate-size group meetings with community leaders to formulate the agenda. These meetings require distribution of background materials, which participants should read prior to the group meetings. In 1994, the Civic Literacy Project, which implemented this idea, used *Interwoven Destinies: Cities and The Nation* edited by Henry Cisneros (1993).

STEP 3: In May of election year, hold a final meeting with community leaders to approve the issue agenda. It is important to achieve consensus (not unanimous agreement) on the final report. The report should articulate issues and solutions that are high priority for the participants.

STEP 4: In June of election year, organize candidate interviews for important primary elections. The goal is not to endorse candidates, but simply to publicize candidate position and group evaluation of the issues so that **voters** can come to **their own** conclusions.

STEP 5: During September and October of election year, organize and hold job interview meetings with candidates for office. Throughout this activity you must be sure to record and report on who participated and what conclusions various meetings reached. Since the purpose is to provide voters with information, you will want to disseminate the interviews widely as a critical component of this activity.

STEP 6: You and classmates will survey a wide variety of local organizations to determine the effectiveness of this educational effort. Candidate organization, political party, and interest group views are solicited in order to improve this activity in future elections. A population survey would be ideal to determine the overall impact of this activity.

You will develop various skills by participating in these projects. In the process, you will learn how to invite candidates to appear; how to use the appearance to educate voters; how to ask questions so that specific and relevant answers are given; how to organize the interview; how to mobilize an audience and have the event carried on cable TV and radio; and how to attract additional media attention for the event.

CHAPTER 8

Citizen Skills

Praxis is the Greek word for combining thought and action. In previous chapters, we have used thought concerning key elements of the political process to introduce you to actions and activities designed to develop key civic literacy skills. In this chapter, we review the civic literacy skills, and from these skills develop a theory of citizen empowerment.

This book is about democratic survival skills. Civic literacy skills are the skills needed for conscious political action. In Chapter 1, we identified a civic component and a literacy component for these skills. The civic component refers to the skills linking citizens with rules used to settle conflicts. Effective political action depends on knowing how and where decisions are made. For example, to participate in elections you need to know who administers elections in your state. The literacy component connects thought and action. Political activity, even watching a TV news program, requires action (turning on the TV) and thought (conscious reflection about the content of the news program).

CIVIC LITERACY SKILLS

Since the key to understanding democratic politics is active learning, we examine the connection between thinking and action. Table 8.1

TABLE 8.1 Civic Literacy Skills

	THINKING SKILLS			
ACTION SKILLS	Awareness	Analysis	Priorities	Advocacy
Commun- ication	discussion	evaluation	agenda setting	argumen- tation
Mobilizing	reaching out	debating	tactics	call to action
Coalition Building	dialogue	strategy	bargaining	selling the idea
Organizing	goal setting	activity plan	assigning tasks	executing
Institution- alizing	stakeholder meetings	capacity assessment	long-range plan	getting sponsors

illustrates how thought and action combine, first to form civic literacy skills, and then to allow citizen empowerment.

This table, by linking thinking and action skills, identifies twenty skills of civic literacy. By following the activities in each chapter, you should by now have become familiar with each of these skills. Over time you will master them. Describing each of these skills in detail helps make you more conscious of having mastered them.

1. Discussion—sharing ideas, concerns, and problems with other people is the first step in understanding how individual problems may be commonly shared and worthy of political action. Talk is fundamental to political action. Articulating the link between personal and public issues is the key to any further political activity. Civic literacy begins with people sharing their views and ideas, first with friends or classmates and then with strangers or students from other courses.

2. Evaluation is a critical step in the politics of linking needs and demands, or problems with solutions. The establishment of causal relationships is necessary to solve public problems. Research reports must clearly identify the connection between means (resources or programs) and ends (goals). Evaluation is used to build support for including issues on agendas and for action plans designed to bring your concerns to the attention of leaders in your community.

3. Agenda setting is a skill that requires deciding which problems warrant the time, attention, and money to be turned into effective demands. Not all worthy and important problems can be solved simultaneously. When there is limited time to speak, time allocations are a function of the importance of the issue and speaker. Conventions that simply accept everyone's suggestion of which issues are important lead to the impression that none of the issues are important.

4. Argumentation—presenting your needs in a clear form—is an essential element of the democratic process. One-sided communication that advocates a particular point of view is a very useful art form in campaigns and interest group lobbying. Talking to other groups or classes in order to convince them that your issue is important requires this skill.

5. Reaching out involves asking another person to become involved in politics. Simply knowing you have been asked to participate in a political activity may put you on the road to other political action. Reaching out implies that a message is received and the need for action is understood (although not always agreed to).

6. Debating is a crucial part of politics, which relies heavily on argumentation and debate as mechanisms to present views and information designed to rally supporters. Political speeches are used primarily to mobilize supporters and only secondarily to convert opponents.

7. Tactics require decisions regarding who to target and what message to deliver. Mobilization efforts must be focused, and energy must be concentrated on activities with the highest payoff. Effective political action requires knowing what precincts can be most effectively canvassed or which groups are likely coalition partners.

8. Call to action is crucial to the process. From Patrick Henry's "Give me liberty or give me death" to Martin Luther King, Jr.'s, "I have a dream," American citizens have been called upon to take political action. Every four years, presidential candidates mobilize citizens to action during the election process. The purpose of any candidate campaign is not just an opportunity to advocate for various policies. Instead, the campaign must advocate in a way that will produce behavior on the part of citizens (voting). Chapter 5 discussed the capacity of "hot cognitions," which are issues closely related to action, and to mobilizing citizens to action.

9. Dialogue requires listening to other people's needs. The first step in reaching an agreement is to listen to the other side's point of view and to articulate your position clearly to the other side. Each side in a negotiation must give and receive information about the needs of potential partners. When diverse groups come together to discuss issues, they can find common ground. Pollster Frank Luntz reports focus groups of 20- and 50-year-olds discussed, and came to consensus on Medicare when both sides agreed to pay more for elderly health care (Klein, 1995).

10. Strategy must be considered before the negotiations start. You will need to think through how to respond under alternative situations. What will you do if the other side. . . ? The basic question here is how you can achieve a partnership that will bring others into a coalition.

11. Bargaining occurs when both sides in a negotiation know what they want most and then seek to create win-win situations where all sides get what they want most. Without priorities, agreement is more difficult, if not impossible. One bit of advice from bargaining experts is to start with the issues about which there is agreement, or which both sides rate as low-priority items (Gustafuson, 1992). This is a common procedure in the Urban Agenda process that was discussed in Chapter 2.

12. Selling the idea takes place once an agreement is struck. At this point, all parties become responsible for selling it to their own members and allies. Leaders can be put in difficult positions selling agreements that represent only part of their demands (see Lipsky, 1968). Getting resolutions of support from other groups, units of government, or individuals is essential.

13. Goal setting is essential because in order for a group or organization to exist, goals must be shared. Goals and tasks must be articulated and agreed upon. Determining how many people are expected for a convention, which groups should be targeted for inclusion in a coalition, or how many voters can be registered, is the first step in the planning process.

14. Activity plan is represented by each of the projects outlined in this book. The activity plan outlines how the activity will be conducted. Scenario building, thinking through logistics, and putting aside unreasonable goals are all part of this component. An example of this skill is the selection of areas for voter registration drives. Using previous turnout statistics and demographic characteristics each area can be prioritized for voter registration canvassing.

15. Assigning tasks is the stage at which the plan is operationalized. The organization's priorities are translated into staff assignments. Assignments must match resources to priorities, with the most valuable people assigned the most important tasks. Assigning workers to specific areas during voter registration drives or managing convention logistics requires an effective allocation of personnel to numerous simultaneous tasks.

16. Execution is getting the job done. A central feature of this skill is making sure people are committed to the task they are assigned and that the task is carried out. Voter registration drives can be elaborately planned, but if people don't actually go and talk to people, there will be no new registrations.

17. Stakeholder meetings are crucial to success. Institutionalization begins with the awareness that long-range needs are not being met under current conditions. A successful voter education campaign will not survive from one election to another without attention to long-term problems and an understanding of what worked and what failed.

18. Capacity assessment is research on organizational strengths and weakness. It is vital to understanding how to improve organizational capacity. Causal relationships must establish how various organizational goals can be achieved.

19. Long-range plans require thinking strategically about the future. Mission statements are a vehicle for articulating long-range priorities and goals.

20. Lobbying involves selling the long-term plan and mission of the organization to partners, sponsors, and collaborators.

Each of these skills is fundamental for effective citizenship. These skills are all present in the activities outlined in the first seven chapters of this book. By reviewing these skills here, you can become more aware of the political activities that link thought and action.

The core concepts of civic literacy require becoming aware of political concerns, creating an environment in which these views are shared, communicating and finding common ground with diverse political and cultural groups, understanding the political institutions and processes that structure political action, and taking planned political action. Citizen empowerment depends on understanding and acting on these concepts. When these concepts are understood and acted upon, civic literacy skills and citizen power are increased.

The four elements of civic literacy are opinions, deliberation, knowledge, and participation.

Opinions are ideas and views about political issues and people. The first step in building an opinion is simply awareness of a specific need to which the political system should respond. Opinions are nurtured by providing opportunities to think about your concerns and problems.

Deliberation is discussion with a purpose. Sharing concerns in a meeting in order to build consensus for a program is an example of deliberation. Deliberation is facilitated by: forming discussion groups with fellow citizens or students; talking to possible coalition partners; and asking citizens to register and vote.

Knowledge, or systematic thinking, is fostered by activities requiring research, policy analysis, planning, and evaluation.

Participation is collective political action. Examples are attending an agenda convention, building a coalition, registering voters, educating voters, mobilizing voters and establishing public accountability.

Civic literacy skills can be taught in a wide variety of settings ranging from educational institutions (at the middle school, high school, and college levels), civic and neighborhood groups, political parties, special interest groups, protest groups, and single-issue advocates. Although educational institutions are mandated and paid by society to provide this service, they have abrogated their responsibility by teaching information—not skills. Increasingly, the training of citizens in the skills of civic literacy has fallen to civic and special interest groups. By articulating the skills necessary for citizenship, we hope to promote their transmission to a new generation of citizens in a wide variety of settings.

Civic literacy requires both thought and action. Thinking skills capture how ideas are processed and action skills are what is done. The thinking skills are awareness, analysis, priority, and advocacy. The action skills are talking and writing (communication), mobilizing, bargaining and coalition building, organizing, and institutionalizing. The building of civic literacy is dependent on understanding and nurturing these skills.

THINKING SKILLS

Awareness

Having a concern or an opinion on any issue is the first step toward moving the political system. You have to know you want something that should be on the government's agenda. Knowledge about who gets what, when, where, and how is also vitally important for citizenship. Understanding the process of government is the ability to answer the when, where, and how questions. Answering these questions requires facts about the process of government (how to get things done), the structure of government (where to get something accomplished), and the policy of government (what is being done). Such information is necessary if citizens are going to influence public decisions. What government does is public policy, and knowledge of policy action and inaction is critical information for activities such as agenda building, coalition building, and evaluating the actions of elected officials. Equally important is each citizen's knowledge of how his or her needs are affected by policy decisions and the creation of political issues.

Choosing Priorities

An essential political skill is the ability to establish priorities. This skill is often referred to as goal articulation, preference articulation, or social choice. It is the ability to articulate priorities among competing issues, interests or values. Recent leadership books by Stephen Covey, 1989, 1994, refer to this ability as "putting first things first." Presidential leadership studies use the term "strategic competency" because the most important decision a president makes is determining which issues and decisions are worth spending time on (Nelson, 1990).

Analysis

This skill requires citizens to first break down complex programs into their component parts and then to understand the relationships between components. For example, an analysis of the health care issue requires examination of the roles and relationships of payers, providers of service, patients, employers, and governmental agencies. The purpose of analysis is the establishment of causal relationships that connect means and ends. Articulating solutions to agreed-upon goals is a necessary step to influencing public policy. In health care, the goal might be to provide universal access. The means to that goal can be providing private health insurance, public health insurance, or the establishment of a national health service that would provide the care directly. Analysis of this issue requires weighing the alternatives and choosing one solution over the others.

Advocacy

Advocacy is the ability to articulate a point of view in a way that is visible and convincing to others. This skill combines articulation, having a point of view, and understanding how to communicate with other elements of the electorate and elected officials. If your analysis convinces you that registration of voters in welfare and unemployment offices should be encouraged, then you need to either convince legislators to change state laws or recruit workers in these offices to register voters.

ACTION SKILLS

Mobilization

Mobilization is recruiting people to act politically. Activities such as getting friends to come to a convention, registering voters, and getting voters to the polls on election day are simple tests of this skill. A more complex test of this skill is getting people to advocate for your issues during the next phase of the agenda convention.

Coalition Building

This is the art and skill of making a deal. Negotiation, compromise, and consensus building are components of this skill. Coalition building skills, both externally and internally, are stressed in the convention and voter mobilization projects.

Organization

The key elements of this skill are planning and coordinating activity toward accomplishing specific tasks. Holding an issue convention requires massive organizational skills in order to coordinate functions such as media relations, speakers, refreshments, publicity, parking, and attendance so that all of the elements are in place at the appropriate time. Voter registration drives require organizing a strategic plan, logistical support for the activities, and monitoring mechanisms.

Institution Building

This is designed to build the long-term capacity of an organization to survive and carry out its mission. Building the long-term capacity of an organization means developing a strategic plan and an action plan to implement the strategic plan. While organizational skills are devoted to short-range goals and projects, this skill places emphasis on long-range problems and opportunities. Examples of institution building are: preparing grant applications to evaluate systematically an organization's projects, acquiring and organizing data resources to facilitate future projects, and lobbying constituencies for future support.

In our democracy, individual or group political power is derived from a process where issues are articulated and prioritized, people are brought together, voters are mobilized, and actions are evaluated. Citizen skills are the building blocks necessary for this process to function

ACTIVE EDUCATION IN CIVIC LITERACY AND CITIZENSHIP

Since both democracy and the acquisition of civic literacy skills require an educational environment and an educational process, we wish to conclude this book with a brief analysis of our experience with these two critical factors.

Nearly every middle school, high school, college, and university has a required course on Introduction to American Government, Civics, or Social Issues. Teachers are trained, hired, and assigned to teach these courses. Students have them as graduation requirements. The infrastructure and resources for the teaching and learning of civic literacy are thus in place. In addition, there are many teachers who have developed their own innovations for bringing civic literacy skills development into these courses. On the other hand, the massive increase in information and analytic models in political science, and their introduction into the textbooks and syllabi of these courses, have greatly reduced the time available for the thought and action skills essential to civic literacy and thus citizen empowerment. An additional factor needs to be taken into consideration when developing a strategy for bringing civic literacy skills back into the curriculum. This factor is the growth of the community service and youth leadership movements in both secondary and postsecondary education.

Just as the movement that created secondary and postsecondary education had as one of its two main goals the creation of educated citizens, which is essential for a civic society, a movement in more modern times has created an educational infrastructure in most secondary and postsecondary institutions for community service and youth leadership development. The combination of these two concepts, civic literacy and community service, is not only feasible at this time, but should it occur, it would have the potential of making our society civically literate.

A principal goal for our political activity requirement is to make students interested in political participation. In this context, student reaction to the project should be assessed on two dimensions: 1.) Was the project a worthwhile educational activity? and 2.) Did the project have any impact on a student's expectations about future political activity?

In order to assess student reaction, we surveyed 286 students who participated in a course with political activities. As a control group, we also surveyed 32 students who were registered for Introduction to American Government (Political Science 101) courses at Wayne State University that did not require the political activities discussed in this handbook.

Student reaction was very positive. Eighty-seven percent (n=250) of the students answered "yes" when asked, "Would you recommend having a similar political activity project the next time this course is offered?" Conversely, when asked if the activity was a waste of time, only 16.8 percent said "yes."

The majority of students felt the amount of time required for the political activity was about right (63.3 percent). Almost 30 percent (28.3 percent) responded that the amount of time spent on the project was too much and 8.4 percent responded the time was too little. These results reflect the student enthusiasm observed during the voter registration drives and issue conventions.

One student criticism of the course organization that emerged from our survey is on the issue of how much of the grade should be based on the political activity project. At the time of the survey, a student could earn up to 40 percent of his/her grade through the activities portion of the course. Almost 65 percent of the students (64.8 percent) thought the project should constitute twenty-five percent or less of their grade. The remaining 35 percent felt the project should count for more than 40 percent of their grade.

The most critical question is whether the students who have participated in the political activity are more or less likely than other political science students to engage in political activity during or after the course. To answer this question, we compare the responses of students in the project with the control group.

In order to gauge political activity, we asked students a series of questions including: whether or not they voted in the Michigan presidential primary election, which occurred during the semester the course was offered; whether they expected to engage in political activity after the course ended; and whether they would ever work in an election campaign.

Table 8.2 compares the responses of students involved in the political activity project with students who were not part of the project. Several cautions are necessary in interpreting these responses. First, the classes that used the political activity project were large, while the control group classes tended to be smaller. Second, as a result of smaller control group classes, the control group was much smaller than the group of students who participated in the project. Third, students were not randomly assigned to the groups in Table 8.2, nor were the classes chosen randomly for inclusion in the political activity project. These cautions mean the results in Table 8.2 must be treated with care.

As Table 8.2 indicates, there is a slight tendency for students in political activity classes to more frequently report voting in the Michigan primary election (45.5 percent for participants and 31.3 percent for the control group). This difference is a disappointment given the class emphasis on voter registration/voter education in conjunction with the Michigan presidential primary. There is even less difference between control and participant groups on whether students will engage in campaign activity in the future.

When asked the less specific question about further political activity, project participants were more likely to view themselves as participating in politics in the future (58.4 percent for project participants compared to 37.7 percent for the control group).

TABLE 8.2 Political Activity Project Participation by Reported and Expected Political Activity

	Percent Responding Yes for Each Political Activity	
	Political Activity Project Participants (N=286)	Control Group (N=32)
Reported and Expected Political Activity		
A. Did you vote in the Michigan Primary on March 17, 1992?	45.5%	31.3%
B. Do you expect to engage in any further political activity after this course is over?	58.4%	37.5%
C. Do you think you will ever work in an election campaign?	38.9%	31.3%

We conclude from these results that the political activity involved in the course work increases the probability of future political activity. Mobilizing others to political activity is the first priority for citizen empowerment.

This book is about building citizen power. We have mapped out strategies and processes to guide you into political action. Ultimately you must choose to become politically active and map out your own course.

References

Aaron, Henry J., Thomas E. Mann, and Timothy Taylor (eds). 1994. *Values and Public Policy*. Washington, DC: The Brookings Institution.

Abramowitz, Alan I. 1988. "Explaining Senate Election Outcomes." *American Political Science Review*, 82:385.

Agranoff, Robert. 1976. *The Management of Election Campaigns*. Boston, MA: Holbrook Press.

Anton, Thomas. 1989. *American Federalism and Public Policy: How the System Works*. New York: Random House.

Asher, Herbert B. 1988. *Presidential Elections and American Politics* (4th ed.) Chicago, IL: Dorsey Press.

Baron, David P. 1994. "Electoral Competition with Informed and Uninformed Voters," *American Political Science Review*, 88:33.

Baumgartner, Frank R., and Bryan D. Jones. 1993. *Agendas and Instability in American Politics*. Chicago, IL:University of Chicago Press.

Berelson, Bernard R., Paul F. Lazarsfeld, and William N. McPhee. 1954. *Voting: A Study of Opinion Formation in a Presidential Campaign*. Chicago, Il: University of Chicago Press.

Berry, Jeffrey M., Kent E. Portney, and Ken Thomson. 1993. *The Rebirth of Urban Democracy*. Washington, DC: The Brookings Institution.

Bibby, John. 1987. *Politics, Parties, and Elections in America*. Chicago,IL: Nelson-Hall.

Burns, J.M., J.W. Pelteson, T.E. Cronin and D.B. Magelby, 1993. *Government by the People*. Englewood Cliffs, N.J.: Prentice Hall.

Campbell, Angus, Philip E. Converse, Warren E. Miller, and Donald E. Stokes, 1960. *The American Voter*. New York: John Wiley and Sons.

_____. 1966. *Elections and the Political Order*. New York: John Wiley and Sons.

Carmines, Edward, and James Stimpson. 1980. "The Two Faces of Issue Voting," *American Political Review*, 74:78.

Carter, Jimmy. 1992. *Turning Point*. New York: Times Books.

Chasnow, Jo-Anne. 1995. *A Preliminary Report on the Impact of the National Voter Registration Act*. New York: HumanSERVE.

Chesney, James. 1994. "Intergovernmental Politics in the Allocation of Block Grant Funds for Substance Abuse in Michigan," *Publius: The Journal of Federalism*, 24:1.

Cisneros, Henry G. 1993. *Interwoven Destinies: Cities and The Nation*. New York: W.W. Norton and Co.

Clinton, Bill. 1992. "The Clinton Health Plan." *The New England Journal of Medicine*, September 10, 1992, p. 804.

Cobb, Roger W., and Charles D. Elder. 1972. *Participation in American Politics: the Dynamics of Agenda-Building*. Baltimore,MD: The Johns Hopkins University Press.

Cohen, Cathy J., and Michael C. Dawson. 1993. "Neighborhood Poverty and African American Politics," *American Political Science Review*, 87:286.

Coleman, James. 1957. *Community Conflict*. Glencoe, IL: Free Press.

Converse, Phillip E. 1964. "The Nature of Belief Systems among Mass Publics," in David Apter (ed.) *Ideology and Discontent*. New York: Free Press, pp.206-61.

Converse, Phillip E., and Gregory B. Markus. 1979. "Plus A Change . . .: The New CPS Election Study Panel," *American Political Science Review*, 73:40.

Covey, Stephen R. 1989. *The 7 Habits of Highly Effective People*. New York: Simon & Schuster.

Covey, Stephen R., D. Roger Merrill, and Rebecca Merrill. 1994. *First Things First*. New York: Simon & Schuster.

Conway, M. Margaret. 1991. *Political Participation in the United States* (2nd ed.) Washington,DC: Congressional Quarterly Press.

Council of State Governments. 1980. *Book of the States*. Lexington, KY.

Ehrenhalt, Alan. 1992. *The United States of Ambition: Politicians, Power and the Pursuit of Office*. New York: Times Books.

Eldersveld, Samuel. 1956. "Experimental Propaganda Techniques and Voting Behavior," *American Political Science Review*, 50 (March 1956) 154-165.

_____ 1964. *Political Parties: A Behavioral Analysis*. Chicago,IL: Rand McNally and Company.

Erikson, Robert S., Gerald C. Wright, and John P. McIver. 1993. *Statehouse Democracy: Public Opinion and Policy in the American States*. New York: Cambridge University Press.

Eulau, Heinz, and Kenneth Prewitt. 1973. *Labyrinths of Democracy: Adaptations, Linkages, Represenation, and Policies in Urban Politics*. Indianapolis, IN: Bobbs-Merrill Company.

Feinstein, Otto. 1993. "America's Urban Agenda: Quo Vadis? Does the American Political Process Still Work?" *Journal of Ethno-Developement*, 3:35.

Fenno, Richard. 1978. *Home Style: House Members and Their Districts.* Glenview, IL: Scott, Foresman.

_____. 1989. *The Making of a Senator: Dan Quayle.* Washington, DC: Congressional Quarterly Press.

_____. 1991. *The Emergence of a Senate Leader: Pete Domenici and the Reagan Budget.* Washington, DC: C Q Press

Fiorina, Morris. 1981. *Retrospective Voting in American National Elections.* New Haven, CT: Yale University Press.

Fischer, David Hackett. 1989. *Albion's Seed: Four British Folkways in America.* New York: Oxford University Press.

Gamson, William. 1992. *Talking Politics.* New York: Cambridge University Press.

Goffman, Bernard, Sheldon Wolin, Peter Euben, Josiah Oben, Arlene Saxenhouse, and Michael Clark. 1994. "The 2500 Anniversary of Democracy: Lessons from Athenian Democracy," *PS: Political Science and Politics,* 26:471.

Goldenberg, Edie N., and Michael W. Traugott. 1984. *Campaigning for Congress.* Washington, DC: Congressional Quarterly Press.

Gosnell, Harold F. 1927. *Getting Out the Vote: An Experiment in the Stimulation of Voting.* Chicago, IL:. University of Chicago Press.

Gray, Virginia, Herbert Jacob, and Robert Albritton. 1990. *Politics in the American States: A Comparative Analysis* (5th ed.) Glencoe, IL: Scott, Foresman.

Gustafuson, David H., William L. Cats-Baril, and Farrokh Alemi. 1992. *Systems to Support Health Policy Analysis: Theory, Models, and Uses.* Ann Arbor, MI: Health Administration Press.

Gutman, Amy. 1987. *Democratic Education.* Princeton, NJ: Princeton University Press.

Hanna, John, Jr. 1991. *The New Texas Early Voting Law.* Austin, TX: Office of the Secretary of State.

Huckfeldt, Robert, and John Sprague. 1992. "Political Parties and Electoral Mobilization: Political Structure, Social Structure, and the Party Canvass" *American Political Science Review,* 86.

Human SERVE. 1995. *Press Release: Moter Voter Registers Hundreds of Thousands in the First Months of 1995.* New York: Human SERVE. March 29,1995.

Ingram, Helen, and Steven Rathgeb (eds.). 1993. *Public Policy for Democracy.* Washington, DC: The Brookings Institution.

Jackson, Robert. 1993. "Voter Mobilization in the 1986 Midterm Election," *Journal of Politics,* 55:1081.

Jacobs, Lawrence R., and Robert Y. Shapiro. 1994. "Studying Substantive Democracy," *PS: Political Science and Politics,* 27:9.

Jenkins, J. Craig. 1985 *The Politics of Insurgency: The Farm Workers Movement in the 1960s.* New York: Columbia University Press.

Johnson, James. 1993. "Is Talk Really Cheap? Promoting a Conversation between Critical Theory and Rational Choice," *American Political Science Review,* 87:75.

Jones, Bryan. 1989. *Leadership and Politics.* Lawrence, KS: University of Kansas Press.

Kinder, Donald, and Ableson, Robert. 1981. "Appraising Presidential Candidates: Personality and Affect in the 1980 Campaign." Paper delivered at the annual meeting of the American Political Association, Sept. 3–6, 1981.

Klein, Joe. "Stalking the Radical Middle," *Newsweek*, September 25, 1995.

Levine, Myron A. *Presidential Campaigns and Elections: Issues, Images, and Partisanship.* Itasca, IL: F.E. Peacock Publishers, Inc.

Lipsky, Michael. 1968. "Protest As a Political Resource," *American Political Science Review*, 62:1151.

MacKuen, Michael, Robert Erikson, and James Stimson 1992. "Peasants or Bankers? The American Electorate and the U.S. Economy." *American Political Science Review*, 86:597.

Maisel, L. Sandy. 1993. *Parties and Elections in America: The Electoral Process.* New York: McGraw-Hill.

McDonagh, Eileen Lorenzi. 1992. "Representative Democracy and State Building in the Progressive Era," *American Political Science Review*, 86:938

Milbrath, Lester. 1965. *Political Participation.* Chicago, IL: Rand McNally.

Miller, Warren E., and Donald E. Stokes. 1963. "Constituency Influence in Congress," *American Political Science Review*, 57:54-56.

National Clearing House on Election Administration, Federal Election Commission. 1993. *Implementing the National Voter Registration Act of 1993: Requirements, Issues, Approaches, and Examples.* Washington, DC:Federal Election Commission.

Nelson, Michael. 1990. *The Presidency and the Political System.* Washington,DC: Congressional Quarterly Press.

Olson, Mancur. 1965. *The Logic of Collective Action.* Cambridge, MA: Harvard University Press.

O'Neill, Tip. 1994. *All Politics Is Local: and Other Rules of the Game.* New York: Times Books.

Page, Benjamin I., and Robert Y. Shapiro. 1992. *The Rational Public: Fifty Years of Trends in Americans' Policy Preferences.* Chicago, Il: University of Chicago Press.

Page, Benjamin. 1994. "Democratic Responsiveness: Untangling the Links between Public Opinion and Policy," *PS: Political Science and Politics*, 27:25.

Pattison, Robert. 1982. *On Literacy: The Politics of Word from Homer to the Age of Rock.* New York: Oxford University Press.

Piven, Frances Fox, and Richard A. Cloward. 1977. *Poor People's Movements: Why They Succeed and How They Fail.* New York: Pantheon Books.

_____. 1988. *Why Americans Don't Vote.* New York: Pantheon Books.

Popkin, Samuel L. 1991. *The Reasoning Voter: Communication and Persuasion in Presidential Campaigns.* Chicago,IL: University of Chicago Press.

Powell, Bingham. 1986 "American Voter in Comparative Perspective," *American Political Science Review*, 80:38.

Putnam, Robert D. 1993. *Making Democracy Work: Civic Traditions in Modern Italy.* Princeton, NJ: Princeton University Press.

Quirk, Paul and Dalager, Jon. 1993. "The Election: a 'New Democrat' and a New Kind of Presidential Campaign," in Nelson, Michael. *The Elections of 1992*. Washington, DC: Congressional Quarterly Press.

Rosenstone, Steven, and John Mark Hansen. 1993. *Mobilization, Participation, and Democracy in America*. New York: Macmillan Publishing Company.

Rossi, Peter and Howard Freeman. 1982. *Evaluation: A Systematic Approach*. Beverly Hills, CA: Sage Publications.

Schattschneider, E.E. 1960. *The Semi-Sovereign People*. New York: Holt, Rinehart and Winston.

Schneider, Anne, and Ingram, Helen. 1993. "Social Construction of Target Populations: Implications for Politics and Policy", *American Political Review*, 87:334.

Skocpol, Theda. 1994. "From Social Security to Health Security? Opinion and Rhetoric in U.S. Social Policy Making," *PS: Political Science and Politics*, 27:21.

Stimson, James A. 1991. *Public Opinion in America: Moods Cycles and Swings*. Boulder, CO: Westview Press.

Stimson, James A., Michael MacKuen, and Robert S. Erikson. 1994. "Opinion and Policy: A Global View," *PS: Political Science and Politics*, 27:29.

Stokes, Donald, and DiLulio, John. 1993. "The Setting: Valence Politics in Modern Elections" in Nelson, Michael, *The Elections of 1992*. Washington, DC: Congressional Quarterly Press.

Sullivan, Louis. 1992. "The Bush Health Plan." *New England Journal of Medicine*, September 10, 1992, p. 802.

Teixeira, Ruy A. 1992. *The Disappearing American Voter*. Washington, DC: The Brookings Institution.

Tilly, Charles. 1978. *From Mobilization to Revolution*.Reading, MA: Addison-Wesley.

Verba, Sidney, Kay Lehman Schlozman, Henry Brady, and Norman H. Nie. 1993. "Citizen Activity: Who Participates? What Do They Say? *American Political Science Review*, 87:303.

Walker, Jack L. 1966. "A Critique of the Elitist Theory of Democracy." *American Political Science Review*, 60:285.

_____. 1991. *Mobilizing Interest Groups in America: Patrons, Professions, and Social Movements*. Ann Arbor, MI: University of Michigan Press.

Weilhouwer, Peter, W., and Brad Lockerbie. 1994. "Party Contacting and Political Participation, 1952–90," *American Journal of Political Science*. 38:211.

Wiessberg, Herbert, and Jerrold Rusk. 1970. "Dimensions of Candidate Evaluations," *American Political Science Review*, 64:1167.

Wills, Garry. 1994. "What Makes a Good Leader?" *Atlantic Monthly*," April, 1994.

Wilson, James Q. 1993. "The Moral Sense: Presidential Address, American Political Association," *American Political Review*. 87:1.

Wolfinger, Raymond, and Steven Rosenstone. 1980. *Who Votes*. New Haven, CT: Yale University Press.

URBAN AGENDA
CONVENTION

SATURDAY, APRIL 9, 1994
GENERAL LECTURES BUILDING

WAYNE STATE UNIVERSITY

URBAN AGENDA CONVENTION PROGRAM
APRIL 9, 1994

9:00- 10:00	Opening Plenary Session Convention Chair: Guest Speakers:	100 General Lectures Prof. Otto Feinstein Margaret Betts, M.D. Detroit Board of Education Prof. James Chesney Wayne State University Mr. James Leidlein City Manager, Harper Woods Judge Adam Shakoor Former Detroit Deputy Mayor Germaine Strobel Michigan Ethnic Heritage Studies Center Roy Levy Williams Chrysler Motor Co. Judge Robert Ziolowski Detroit Recorder's Court
	Keynote Address:	George Cushingberry, Jr. Wayne County Commissioner
10:00- 12:00	Small Workshops (See page 4 for complete listings)	Manoogian Building
12:00	LUNCH BREAK	
1:00- 3:00	Student Caucuses (See page 5 for classroom assignments)	Manoogian Building
4:00- 5:00	Closing Plenary Session	100 General Lectures

The rules of order for the convention will be moved and voted on in the opening plenary session, and the resolution proposal to be submitted for voting later in the day will be read as well. The proposed rules are printed on page 3 of this program; the full text of the resolution proposal is on pages 6-7. The final vote on the resolution, and any changes to be made, will occur in the closing plenary session beginning at 4:00.

URBAN AGENDA CONVENTION: PROPOSED RULES

The rules will be proposed and voted on at the 9-10 a.m. plenary session.

1. The Urban Agenda Resolution will be read at the 9-10 a.m. plenary session and presented for consideration and vote at the 3-4 p.m. plenary session.

2. The rules will be read at the 3-4 p.m. plenary session to remind the participants of the rules under which they are operating.

4. The Urban Agenda Resolution must be moved and seconded by six (6) sections (with a majority of support in each section) to be placed on the floor.

5. Once this has been done at the 3-4 p.m. plenary session, each major issue will be discussed (90 seconds pro and 90 seconds con) *ad seriatum* (one by one). To remain on the agenda an issue must receive a majority vote of those voting.

6. Once the issues on the agenda have been voted up or down, new issues can be considered if they have majority support in six (6) sections. They will then be discussed (90 seconds pro and 90 seconds con) and then voted on. To be accepted such an issue must have a majority vote of those voting.

7. Those issues receiving a majority vote of those voting will make up the Winter Term 1994 Urban Agenda.

8. If the majority on a voice vote is not clear, the chair may call for a hand count. If it is still not clear, a roll call by course sections can be requested.

9. A motion to adjourn has precedence over other motions.

10. Points of procedural order only may be raised from the floor, by raising one's hand for recognition.

11. Those wishing to speak on an agenda issue must line up behind one of the floor microphones.

CAUCUS SESSION ROOMS

Students Will Meet Together With Their Guests, and Section Classmates from 1:00 To 3:00 In The Afternoon, Using The Classrooms Assigned Below. Note: All Sections Will Be Meeting In The Manoogian Building, Except For John Lees' Sections, Which Will All Meet In Room 175 Of General Lectures.

Room	Caucus		
266	Mon. 8:30	Discussion	(Tony and Jocelyn)
68	Mon. 8:30	Discussion	(Jay)
256	Tues. 8:30	Discussion	(Jay and Steffanie)
201	Tues. 9:35	Discussion	(Tony and Peter)
205	Tues. 9:35	Discussion	(Cynthia and Liz)
171	Tues. 10:40	Discussion	(Tony and Keith)
225	Thurs. 9:35	Discussion	(Cynthia and Charles)
65	Fri. 10:40	Discussion	(Cynthia)
275	Fri. 11:45	Discussion	(Jay and Brian)
289		PS 101 Tu/Th	Prof. Jim Chesney
293		PS 101 M/Tu/W/Th	Jeff Farrah
280		PS 103 Fri.	Prof. Ray Johnston
211		PS 224 Wed	Prof. Feinstein
259		Jordan College	Prof. Carter Stevenson
221	Martin Luther King High School		
269	Southeast Michigan American Assembly		
243	Detroit City Council Youth Commission		

All Detroit city residents who are interested in becoming deputy registrars for the city are welcome to participate in an April 21st training and swearing-in by the City clerk's office. Date: Thursday, April 21. Time: 4:00 p.m. Location: Detroit City County Building, 2 Woodward Avenue, 13th floor auditorium. This activity is being coordinated by the Detroit City Council Youth Commission.

WORKSHOPS

Each Of The Workshops Listed Below Will Be Held For Two 55-Minute Sessions. The First Session Will Last From 10:00-10:55; The Second Session Will Last From 11:00-11:55. All Rooms Listed Are In The Manoogian Building.

Room	Workshop
266	Education: Finance Issues
68	Education: Quality, Curriculum, Staffing
256	Education: School Environment & Safety
201	Children at Risk: Child Abuse
205	Children at Risk: Substance Abuse
171	Children at Risk: Teenage Pregnancy
212	Children at Risk: Gangs
218	Economics: Jobs
225	Economics: Poverty and Homelessness
253	Economics: Welfare Reform
65	Economics: Community Development & Infrastructure
275	Crime and Violence: Prison Reform
289	Crime and Violence: Media & Prevention Issues
293	Crime and Violence: Gun Control
243	Crime and Violence: Hate Crimes
280	Justice: Violence Against Women
259	Multicultural Society
221	Health Care
269	Environment
75	Family

Room	Time	Workshop
262*	10:00-11:00	Urban Student Self-Help: Books
	11:00-12:00	Urban Student Self-Help; Day Care
211*	10:00-11:00	MLK, Jr. Saturday School: Civic Literacy
	11:00-12:00	Mentoring Program for Urban Children
226*	10:00-11:00	The U.S. Constitution as a Multicultural Tool
	11:00-12:00	Comparing U.S. & European Multicultural Policy
297*	11:00-12:00	Urban, Bi-lingual, Multicultural Education

*Sessions held in these rooms will be continued during the afternoon period of 1:00-3:00 also.

URBAN AGENDA RESOLUTION PROPOSAL—WINTER 1994

The following six issue areas have been identified by a process originating with student classroom discussions and voting, followed by a process of delegate representation and negotiation. These issue statements are put forward at this time, on April 9, 1994, for a vote of ratification and support by the entire PS l01, class of Prof. Otto Feinstein in the Winter 1994 semester, together with their guests and other students seeking to build an Urban Agenda coalition.

I. EDUCATION
   A. The *quality* of education is low and needs improvement.
   B. *Funding* is inadequate and unequal across districts.
   C. There is too much *violence* in the schools.
   D. Levels of *parent participation* are too low.

II. CRIME AND VIOLENCE
   A. There are 640,000 violent crimes committed with *handguns* annually.
   B. Since 1991, 43,000 convicts who were released from prison early because of *overcrowding* have been rearrested.
   C. There is no agreement between the Senate and the House when it comes to an effective crime bill.
   D. There are no adequate *anti-crime* programs at the junior high and high school levels where murders committed by teens increased by 124%.
   E. There is no effective *rehabilitation* program in the federal prison system.
   F. More *security* and or *police* are needed in urban cities and schools.

III. HEALTH CARE
   A. Roughly 37 million Americans do not have health insurance and many more have inadequate coverage. As a result, access to health care is not universally available.
   B. Plans to promote universal access to health care must not reduce the quality of care and must contain cost increases.
   C. Problems of *access*, *cost*, and *quality of health care* are concentrated in core urban areas. In southeast Michigan these problems are concentrated in Detroit.

IV. SOCIAL WELFARE
   A. There has been an ever increasing rate of *unemployment* as a result of plant closings in the city of Detroit. Unfortunately, unemployment in itself breeds *poverty* stricken families, crime and in some instances even *homelessness.*
   B. *Domestic Violence* on either the spouse or children is a calamity which is very prevalent. Families are often destroyed and in some instances death is the final result of domestic violence. We have labeled these families, "dysfunctional." Children are shuffled through the foster care system as a result of this problem.

Children are impacted greatly by these sometimes unfit parents and may resort to violent or neglectful behaviors because they never learn how to handle family and/or crisis situations.

C. *Child neglect* is a serious problem in our urban cities which is often the result of unplanned pregnancies. Parents are sometimes unfit to raise a child because of their young age or lack of commitment to the child they have grudgingly been forced to birth. Sadly, it is this problem that is far too often reported under the headlines. "3 Day Old Infant Found in Dumpster." Fathers in some cases abandon the family because they are unable to stay in the home to provide a family unit because of benefits the family may require based on the structure and criteria of Social Services.

D. The Social Welfare system must be reorganized to include the needs of *elderly adults, children, and mentally and physically challenged people* who are without representation in our current system.

V. ECONOMICS

The problems of the economy include the following areas:
A. Trade and budget deficits.
B. Unemployment.
C. Poverty and homelessness.
D. Taxes.
E. Infrastructure.

VI. ENVIRONMENT

A. Air pollution causes respiratory disorders and other human health problems, damages crops and livestock, and damages the earth's atmosphere.

B. By the year 2000, the decrease in the ozone layer will cause 300,000 additional cases of skin cancer, and an additional 1.6 million cases of cataracts.

C. In the near future, American citizens will have to pay more for fruits and vegetables because due to soil pollution plants will grow only in certain areas.

D. Ninety-five percent of California woods have been cut down to make way for development; such cutting affects the habitats and ecosystems of many animals that are important to the survival of humans.

E. Last year, 11 million gallons of oil spilled into waters and killed thousands of animals.

F. The Great Lakes and the Detroit River are regularly threatened by such factors as toxic waste dumping and acid rain. Great care must be taken to preserve these valuable natural resources.

URBAN AGENDA CONVENTION
SATURDAY, APRIL 9, 1994

The Wayne State University Urban Agenda Convention is being broadcast today by satellite link-up to the following colleges and universities:

Wayne County Community College
University of Michigan - Dearborn
Eastern Michigan University
Washtenaw Community College
General Motors Institute

Henry Ford Community College
Schoolcraft Community College
Western Michigan University
Mott Community college
University of Michigan - Flint

The following cable companies will carry broadcasts of the Urban Agenda Convention today and for some, throughout the coming week:

Barden Cable
Booth Communications
Cablevision Industries
Continental Cablevision
Maclean Hunter Cable TV
Meteorvision
Omnicom of Michigan
United Artists Cable Television of Oakland County

The Urban Agenda Project would like to thank the following people for their generous support:

Wayne State University Department of Political Science
WSU President's Affirmative Action Award
Michigan Campus Compact
American Assembly-Columbia University
Michigan Community Service Commission
Michigan Jobs Commission
Barden Cable
Southeast Michigan Television Education Consortium

In November 1994 numerous elections will be held throughout the state of Michigan, including those for the offices of U.S. Senator, U.S. Representative, and Governor. *Are you registered to vote?* Voter registrars will be at a table in the General Lectures lobby throughout the day today; stop by and register! If you have moved and need to update your voter registration address, they are ready and willing to help.

State Election Officials

Alabama

Jerry Henderson
Administrator of Elections
P.O. Box 5616
Montgomery, AL 36103-5616

Alaska

Joe Swanson
Director of Elections
Division of Elections
P.O. Box 110017
Juneau, AK 99811-0017

Arizona

Margaret Stears
State Election Officer
Capitol West Wing
1700 W. Washington
Phoenix, AZ 85007-2808

Arkansas

Rhonda Langster
Supervisor of Elections
Election Services
State Capitol Bldg., Rm. 026
Little Rock, AR 72201

California

Caren Daniels-Meade
Chief
Elections and Political Reform
1230 J Street, Rm. 232
Sacramento, CA 95814

Colorado

Donetta Davidson
Elections Officer
Dept. of State
1560 Broadway, Ste. 200
Denver, CO 80202

Connecticut

Joanne Chrisoulis
Manager, Election Services
30 Trinity Street
Hartford, CT 06106

Delaware

Richard B. Harper
State Election Commissioner
32 Loockerman Square, Ste. 203
Dover, DE 19901

District of Columbia

Emmett H Fremaux, Jr.
Executive Director
Board of Elections and Ethics
1 Judiciary Square, Ste. 250
441 4th Street, N.W.
Washington, DC 20001

Florida

Dorothy W. Joyce
Director
Division of Elections
Dept. of State
The Capitol, Rm. 1801
Tallahassee, FL 32399-0250

Georgia

H. Jeff Lanier
Director, Elections Division
Office of the Secretary of State
State Capitol, Rm. 110
Atlanta, GA 30334

Hawaii

Dwayne Yoshina
Deputy Executive Officer
Election Division
Office of the Lieutenant
    Governor
State Capitol, 5th Fl.
Honolulu, HI 96813

Idaho

Ben Ysursa
Chief Deputy Secretary of State
    for Elections
203 State House
Boise, ID 83720

Illinois

Dr. Ronald Michaelson
Executive Director
State Board of Elections
1020 S. Spring Street
P.O. Box 4187
Springfield, IL 62708

Indiana

David Maidenburg
Executive Director
State Board of Elections
302 W. Washington
Indianapolis, IN 46204

Iowa

Sandy Steinbach
Director of Elections
Office of Secretary of State
Hoover State Office Bldg.
Des Moines, IA 50319

Kansas

Brad Bryant
Deputy Assistant for Elections
    and Legislative Matters
Capitol Bldg.
Topeka, KS 66612

Kentucky

George Russell
Executive Director
State Board of Elections
140 Walnut Street
Frankfort, KY 40601

Louisiana

Jerry Fowler
Commissioner of Elections
4888 Constitution Avenue
P.O. Box 14179
Baton Rouge, LA 70809-4179

Maine

Lorraine M. Fleury
Director of Elections
State House, Sta. 101
Augusta, ME 04333

Maryland

Gene M. Raynor
Administrator
State Administrative Board
P.O. Box 231
Annapolis, MD 21404-0231

Massachusetts

John Cloonan
Director of Elections
Election Division, Rm.1705
Office of the Secretary of the
    Commonwealth
One Ashburton Place
Boston, MA 02108

Michigan

Christopher M. Thomas
Director of Elections
Department of State
Mutual Building, 4th
208 N. Capitol Ave.
Lansing, MI 48901

Mississippi

Constance Slaughter-Harvey
Assistant Secretary of State
P.O. Box 136
Jackson, MS 39205

Missouri

Joe Carroll
Deputy Secretary of State for
    Election Services
MO State Information Center
600 West Main Street
Jefferson City, MO 65101

Montana

Joe Kerwin
Election Bureau Chief
Office of Secretary of State
State Capitol, Rm. 225
Helena, MT 59620

Nebraska

Ralph Englert
Deputy Secretary of State and
Director of Elections
Office of Secretary of State
State Capitol, Ste. 2300
Lincoln, NE 68509

Nevada

Dale Erquiaga
Deputy Secretary of State for
    Elections
Capitol Complex
Carson City, NV 89710

New Hampshire

Karen H. Ladd
Assistant Secretary of State
State House, Rm. 204
Concord, NH 03301

New Jersey

Lillian M. Trainor, Director
Election Division
Dept. of State
315 W. State Street, CN 304
Trenton, NJ 08625-0304

New Mexico

Hoyt Clifton
Director
Bureau of Elections
State Capitol Bldg., 4th Fl.
Santa Fe, NM 87503

New York

Thomas Wilkey
Executive Director
State Board of Elections
One Commerce Plaza
P.O. Box Four
Albany, NY 12260

North Carolina

Gary O. Bartlett
Executive Director
State Board of Elections
P.O. Box 1166
Raleigh, NC 27602

Ohio

Donna Harter
Elections Administrator
Office of Secretary of State
30 E. Broad Street, 14th Fl.
Columbus, OH 43266-0418

Oklahoma

Lance D. Ward
Secretary
State Election Board
3-B State Capitol
P.O. Box 53156
Oklahoma City, OK 73152

Oregon

Colleen Sealock
Director of Elections
Office of Secretary of State
141 State Capitol
Salem, OR 97310

Pennsylvania

William P. Boehm
Commissioner of Elections
305 North Office Bldg.
Harrisburg, PA 17120

Rhode Island

Jan Armstrong
Executive
State Board of Elections
50 Branch Ave.
Providence, RI 02904

South Carolina

James Hendrix
Assistant Executive Director
State Election Commission
P.O. Box 5987
Columbia, SC 29250

South Dakota

Chris Nelson
Supervisor of Elections
State Capitol Bldg., 2nd Fl.
500 E. Capitol
Pierre, SD 57501-5070

Tennessee

Will Burns
Coordinator of Elections
James K. Polk Bldg., Ste. 500
Nashville, TN 37243-0309

Texas

Tom Harrison
Special Assistant for Elections
Office of Secretary of State
P.O. Box 12060
Austin, TX 78711

Utah

Howard Rigtrup
Deputy Lieutenant Governor
State Capitol Bldg., Rm. 203
Salt Lake City, UT 84114

Vermont

Ellen Tofferi
Director of Elections
Office of Secretary of State
Redstone Bldg.
26 Terrace Street
Montpelier, VT 05609-1102

Virginia

Audrey Piatt
Deputy Director
State Board of Elections
200 N. 9th Street, Rm. 101
Richmond, VA 23219-3497

Washington

Gary McIntosh
Election Director
Elections Division
Office of Secretary of State
Legislative Bldg., AS-22
Olympia, WA 98504-0422

West Virginia

William H. Harrington
Chief of Staff
State Capitol, Rm. 157-K
1900 Kanawha Blvd., East
Charleston, WV 25305

INDEX